THE LITERATE CAT

BROWNTROUT PUBLISHERS INC.
SAN FRANCISCO

THE LITERATE CAT
A PHOTOGRAPHIC CELEBRATION

FEATURING QUOTATIONS FROM SHAKESPEARE,
HERODOTUS, BAUDELAIRE, DARWIN, KEATS
AND OTHER FELINE FANCIERS

BROWNTROUT PUBLISHERS INC.
SAN FRANCISCO

)TOGRAPHY/LITERATURE $25.95

THE LITERATE CAT
HOTOGRAPHIC CELEBRATION

100 full color photographs
Hardcover

Entire contents ©1995 BrownTrout Publishers, Inc.
Photography ©1995
Henry Ausloos / Animals Animals
Frank Balthis
G. I. Bernard / Animals Animals
Margot Conte / Animals Animals
E. R. Degginger / Animals Animals
Nicholas Devore III / Photographers Aspen
George F. Godfrey / Animals Animals
Ted Grant / Masterfile
Gerard Lacz / Animals Animals
Robert Maier / Animals Animals
Joe McDonald / Animals Animals
Patti Murray / Animals Animals
Robert Pearcy / Animals Animals
Mike & Moppet Reed / Animals Animals
Reed / Williams / Animals Animals
Ralph A. Reinhold / Animals Animals
L. L. T. Rhodes / Animals Animals
Reneé Stockdale / Animals Animals
A. Thomas / Animals Animals
Alfred B. Thomas / Animals Animals
Sydney Thomson / Animals Animals
Karen Tweedy-Holmes / Animals Animals
Peter Weimann / Animals Animals
Barbara J. Wright / Animals Animals

LIBRARY OF CONGRESS
CATALOGING-IN-PUBLICATION DATA

The literate cat : a photographic celebration : featuring
    quotations from Shakespeare, Herodotus, Baudelaire,
    Darwin, Keats, and other feline fanciers.
        p.   cm.
    ISBN 1-56313-740-2 (hardcover : alk. paper)
    1. Cats—Quotations, maxims, etc. 2. Cats—Pictorial
works.   I. Browntrout Publishers.
PN6084.C23L59   1995   95-37223
808.8'036—dc20   CIP

Printed and bound by
Dai Nippon Printing Company, Ltd., Hong Kong

10 9 8 7 6 5 4 3 2 1

INTRODUCTION

All the animals with which people have had to do have afforded scope to the literary imagination. The warhorse of Job; the watchdog of Odysseus; the dolphin of Dionysus—truly, no creature of fur, fin, or feather, but has been seized on and taken up by the symbol-making faculties of poets and writers. But it is the cat that has most deeply struck the human imagination, that has been most often, and most intensely, the subject of that "shaping spirit." Why should this be? Why is the cat the imaginative creature *par excellence,* the animal most intimately associated with the creative mind, with the imagination, with the faculty by which people both make and understand the world?

The imagination is a combining faculty, one that creates unions, or fusions, of qualities themselves widely remote, or even antithetical. It is the "twice born" faculty, in which every thought or experience comes into being simultaneously with its sensual analogue, or symbol. It refers not to simples, but to unions; not to thought by itself, or experience in isolation, but to the fusion of thought, experience and sense—to totalities, mysterious in themselves but evocative to others; to mysteries, impossible to analyze but equally impossible to resist.

Now of all such subtle and inscrutable experience *the cat* is the natural symbol, for the cat is itself the embodiment of the fusion, or union, of opposite traits, the embodiment of the interpenetration of thought and sense. It is the cat that is both soft and cruel, that possesses "the spring nail in the velvet paw"; it is the cat that is both indifferent and hyperaware, submitting every evanescent and subtle shift in its environment to the audit of its senses, even while it sleeps; it is the cat that keeps an eternal poise between enticement and rebuff, between beauty and savagery, between abstraction and regard; that, even as it leaps forward, has begun to pull back, to withdraw; whose gravity is leavened with whim, and whose play is dead earnest; and all this as an embodiment, a physical and sensual expression; as an immediate and phenomenal analogue to a mystery within at once remote and familiar, wild and contained, impenetrable and irresistible.

Is it any wonder, then, that the cat should so richly furnish the imagination with symbols, when it is itself a symbol—of the imagination? When it embodies that faculty even while it exemplifies its objects and products?

But there is another and perhaps deeper affinity between these two. For the imagination is above all the faculty by which we intuit or touch the lives and experiences of others, by which we overleap the "thick wall of personality" that isolates and impoverishes us. The cat is the most autonomous of creatures, yet no more autonomous than any other living thing; the most sovereign and inward, yet no less susceptible than any other sovereign and inward thing to love and to touch. When we love a cat, and touch its life, we exercise that faculty that could, if so directed, enable us to love others, and to touch their lives as well. And it is here, beyond its aesthetic significance, as an exemplar of all life outside us, yet accessible to us, that the cat gains a moral value of even greater importance.

—*Charles Burke*

THE CAT AND THE RAT

Four creatures, wont to prowl,—
  Sly Grab-and-Snatch, the cat,
  Grave Evil-bode, the owl,
  Thief Nibble-stitch, the rat,
And Madam Weasel, prim and fine,—
Inhabited a rotten pine.
  A man their home discovered there,
And set, one night, a cunning snare.
  The cat, a noted early-riser,
    Went forth, at break of day,
    To hunt her usual prey.
      Not much the wiser
    For morning's feeble ray,
  The noose did suddenly surprise her.
    Waked by her strangling cry,
    Gray Nibble-stitch drew nigh:
    As full of joy was he
    As of despair was she,
    For in the noose he saw
    His foe of mortal paw.
Dear friend, said Mrs. Grab-and-Snatch,
Do, pray, this cursed cord detach.
  I've always known your skill,
  And often your good will;
Now help me from this worst of snares,
In which I fell at unawares.
  'Tis by a sacred right,
    You, sole of all your race,
    By special love and grace,
  Have been my favorite—
    The darling of my eyes.
  'Twas ordered by celestial cares
No doubt; I thank the blessed skies,
  That, going out to say my prayers,
As cats devout each morning do,
This net has made me pray to you.
Come, fall to work upon the cord.
Replied the rat, And what reward
  Shall pay me, if I dare?
  Why, said the cat, I swear
  To be your firm ally:
  Henceforth, eternally,
  These powerful claws are yours,
  Which safe your life insures.
I'll guard from quadruped and fowl;
I'll eat the weasel and the owl.
  Ah, cried the rat, you fool!
I'm quite too wise to be your tool.
He said, and sought his snug retreat,
Close at the rotten pine-tree's feet,
Where plump he did the weasel meet;
Whom shunning by a happy dodge,
He climbed the hollow trunk to lodge;
  And there the savage owl he saw.
  Necessity became his law,
  And down he went, the rope to gnaw.
  Strand after strand in two he bit,
  And freed, at last, the hypocrite.
  That moment came the man in sight;
  The new allies took hasty flight.
    A good while after that,
    Our liberated cat
    Espied her favorite rat,
  Quite out of reach, and on his guard.
My friend, said she, I take your shyness hard,
  Your caution wrongs my gratitude;
    Approach, and greet your stanch ally.
    Do you suppose, darling rat, that I
  Forget the solemn oath I mewed?
  Do I forget, the rat replied,
  To what your nature is allied?
    To thankfulness, or even pity,
    Can cats be ever bound by treaty?

    Alliance from necessity
    Is safe just while it has to be.
                              —LaFontaine

Gerard Lacz /
Animals Animals

Sydney Thomson / Animals Animals

COME, LOVELY PUSS

Come, lovely puss, upon my breast recline;
Do not unsheathe your claws for me to feel
But let me drown within your eyes so fine,
Compounded both of agate and of steel.

And when my fingers lazily caress
Your head, your back spring-loaded like a bow,
My hands so drunk with ecstasy confess
From you to me electric currents flow.

Ah, then in dreams I see my bride, whose glance
Like yours, my lovely puss, so deep and still,
Me pierces to the heart, a very lance
And stings; from head to foot a mystic thrill.
A heady perfume dangerous and rare
From her bronze body floats and scents the air.

— *Le Chat,* Charles Pierre Baudelaire

A FOUR-FOOTED BEASTE

Cats are of divers colours; but for the most part gryseld like to congealed yse, which commeth from the condition of her meate; her head is like unto the head of a Lyon, except in her sharpe eares: her flesh is soft and smooth: her eies glister above measure especially when a man commeth to see a cat on the sudden, and in the night they can hardly be endured for their flaming aspect.

It is a neat and cleanely creature, oftentimes licking hir own body to keepe it smoothe and faire, having naturally a flexible backe for this purpose, and washing hir face with hir fore feet, but some observe that if she put hir feete beyond the crowne of her head, that it is a presage of raine, and if the backe of a cat be thinne, the beast is of no courage or value.

It is needeless to spend any time about her loving nature to man, how she flattereth by rubbing her skinne against ones Legges, how she whurleth with her voyce, having as many tunes as turnes, for she hath one voyce to beg and to complain, another to testifie her delight and pleasure, another among hir own kind by flattring, by hissing, by purring, by spitting, insomuch as some have thought that they have a peculiar intelligible language among themselves.

Therefore, how she beggeth, playeth, leapeth, looketh, catcheth, tosseth with her foote, riseth up to strings held over her head, sometime creeping, sometimes lying on the back, playing with one foote, sometime on the bely, snatching, now with mouth, and anon with foote, apprehending greedily any thing save the hand of a man, with divers such gestical actions, it is needeless to stand upon: insomuch as Coelius was wont to say that being free from his Studies and more urgent waighty affairs, he was not ashamed to play and sport himselfe with a Cat.

—*The Historie of Four-Footed Beastes,* Edward Topsell

AN HUMBLE PETITION PRESENTED
TO MADAME HELVÉTIUS BY HER CATS

We shall not endeavour to defend ourselves equally from devouring as many sparrows, blackbirds, and thrushes, as we can possibly catch. But here we have to plead in extenuation, that our most cruel enemies, your Abbés themselves, are incessantly complaining of the ravages made by these birds among the cherries and other fruit. The Sieur Abbé Morellet, in particular, is always thundering the most violent anathemas against the blackbirds and thrushes, for plundering your vines, which they do with as little mercy as he himself. To us, however, most illustrious Lady, it appears that the grapes may just as well be eaten by *blackbirds* as *Abbés,* and that our warfare against the winged plunderers will be fruitless, if you encourage other biped and feather-less pilferers, who make ten times more havoc.

We know that we are also accused of eating nightingales, who never plunder, and sing, as they say, most enchantingly. It is indeed possible that we may now and then have gratified our palates with a delicious morsel in this way, but we can assure you that it was in utter ignorance of your affection for the species; and that, resembling sparrows in their plumage, we, who make no pretensions to being connoisseurs in music, could not distinguish the song of the one from that of the other, and therefore supposed ourselves regaling only on sparrows. A cat belonging to M. Piccini has assured us, that they who only know how to *mew,* cannot be any judges of the art of singing; and on this we rest for our justification. However, we will henceforward exert our utmost endeavours to distinguish the *Gluckists,* who are, as we are informed, the sparrows, from the *Piccinists,* who are the nightingales. We only intreat of you to pardon the inadvertence into which we may possibly fall, if, in roving after nests, we may sometimes fall upon a brood of *Piccinists,* who, being then destitute of plumage, and not having learnt to sing, we will have no mark by which to distinguish them.

—Benjamin Franklin

Nicholas Devore III / Photographers Aspen

Nicholas Devore III / Photographers Aspen

THE TONGUE

Cultivate your garden, said Goethe and Voltaire,
Every other task is wasted and dead-born;
Narrow all your efforts to a given sphere,
Seek your Heaven daily in a bit of ground.
So my cat behaves. Like a veteran,
He brushes well his coat before he sits to dine;
All his work is centered in his own domain,
Just to keep his spotless fur soft, and clean, and fine.

His tongue is sponge, and brush, and towel, and curry-comb,
Well he knows what work it can be made to do,
Poor little wash-rag, smaller than my thumb.
His nose touches his back, touches his hind paws, too,
Every patch of fur is raked, and scraped, and smoothed;
What more has Goethe done, what more could Voltaire do?
— *"Practice,"* Hippolyte Taine,
translated by Agnes Repplier

Gerard Lacz / Animals Animals

SHE SIGHTS A BIRD

She sights a Bird — she chuckles —
She flattens — then she crawls —
She runs without the look of feet —
Her eyes increase to Balls —

Her Jaws stir — twitching — hungry —
Her Teeth can hardly stand —

She leaps, but Robin leaped the first —
Ah, Pussy, of the Sand,

The Hopes so juicy ripening —
You almost bathed your Tongue —
When Bliss disclosed a hundred Toes —
And fled with every one —

—Emily Dickinson

JOHN MORTONSON'S FUNERAL

John Mortonson was dead: his lines in 'the tragedy of "Man"' had all been spoken and he had left the stage.

The body rested in a fine mahogany coffin fitted with a plate of glass. All arrangements for the funeral had been so well attended to that had the deceased known he would doubtless have approved. The face, as it showed under the glass, was not disagreeable to look upon: it bore a faint smile, and as the death had been painless, had not been distorted beyond the repairing power of the undertaker. At two o'clock of the afternoon the friends were to assemble to pay their last tribute of respect to one who had no further need of friends and respect. The surviving members of the family came severally every few minutes to the casket and wept above the placid features beneath the glass. This did them no good; it did no good to John Mortonson; but in the presence of death reason and philosophy are silent.

As the hour of two approached the friends began to arrive and after offering such consolation to the stricken relatives as the proprieties of the occasion required, solemnly seated themselves about the room with an augmented consciousness of their importance in the scheme funereal. Then the minister came, and in that overshadowing presence the lesser lights went into eclipse. His entrance was followed by that of the widow, whose lamentations filled the room. She approached the casket and after leaning her face against the cold glass for a moment was gently led to a seat near her daughter. Mournfully and low the man of God began his eulogy of the dead, and his doleful voice, mingled with the sobbing which it was its purpose to stimulate and sustain, rose and fell, seemed to come and go, like the sound of a sullen sea. The gloomy day grew darker as he spoke; a curtain of cloud underspread the sky and a few drops of rain fell audibly. It seemed as if all nature were weeping for John Mortonson.

When the minister had finished his eulogy with prayer a hymn was sung and the pallbearers took their places beside the bier. As the last notes of the hymn died away the widow ran to the coffin, cast herself upon it and sobbed hysterically. Gradually, however, she yielded to dissuasion, becoming more composed; and as the minister was in the act of leading her away her eyes sought the face of the dead beneath the glass. She threw up her arms and with a shriek fell backward insensible.

The mourners sprang forward to the coffin, the friends followed, and as the clock on the mantel solemnly struck three all were staring down upon the face of John Mortonson, deceased.

They turned away, sick and faint. One man, trying in his terror to escape the awful sight, stumbled against the coffin so heavily as to knock away one of its frail supports. The coffin fell to the floor, the glass shattered to bits by the concussion.

From the opening crawled John Mortonson's cat, which lazily leapt to the floor, sat up, tranquilly wiped its crimson muzzle with a forepaw, then walked with dignity from the room.

—Ambrose Bierce

Mike & Moppet Reed / Animals Animals

Reneé Stockdale / Animals Animals

'RED SLIPPERS'

A wicked cat, grown old and gray,
That she was a shoemaker chose to say,
And put before her window a board
Where slippers for young maidens were stored;
While some were of morocco made,
Others of satin were there display'd;
Of velvet some, with edges of gold,
And figured strings, all gay to behold.
But fairest of all exposed to view
Was a pair of slippers of scarlet hue;
They gave full many a lass delight
With their gorgeous colours and splendour bright.

A young and snow-white noble mouse
Who chanced to pass the shoemaker's house
First turn'd to look, and then stood still,
And then peep'd over the window sill.
At length she said: 'God day, mother cat;
You've pretty red slippers, I grant you that

If they're not dear, I'm ready to buy,
So tell me the price, if it's not too high.'

'My good young lady,' the cat replied,
'Pray do me the favor to step inside,
And honor my house, I venture to pray,
With your gracious presence. Allow me to say
That the fairest maidens come shopping to me,
And duchesses too, of high degree.
The slippers I'm willing full cheap to sell,
Yet let us see if they'll fit you well.
Pray step inside, and take a seat' –
Thus the wily cat did falsely entreat,
And the poor white thing in her ignorance then
Fell plump in the snare in that murderous den.
The little mouse sat down on a chair,
And lifted her small leg up in the air,
In order to try how the red shoes fitted,
A picture of innocent calm to be pitied.

When sudden the wicked cat seized her fast,
Her murderous talons around her cast,
And bit right off her poor little head.
'My dear white creature,' the cat then said,
'My sweet little mouse, you're as dead as a rat.
The scarlet red slippers that served me so pat
I'll kindly place on the top of your tomb,
And when is heard, on the last day of doom,
The sound of the trump, O mouse so white,
From out of your grave you'll come to light,
Like all the rest, and then you'll be able
To wear your red slippers.' Here ends my fable.

MORAL

Ye little white mice, take care where you go,
And don't be seduced by worldly show;
I counsel you sooner barefooted to walk,
Than buy slippers of cats, however they talk.

—The Poems of Heine,
translated by E. A. Bowring

Barbara J. Wright / Animals Animals

CAT AND KING

A cat was looking at a King, as permitted by the proverb.

"Well," said the monarch, observing her inspection of the royal person, "how do you like me?"

"I can imagine a King," said the Cat, "whom I should like better."

"For example?"

"The King of Mice."

The sovereign was so pleased with the wit of the reply that he gave her permission to scratch his Prime Minister's eyes out.

—Ambrose Bierce

A DOG'S ADVANTAGES

Pussy can sit by the fire and sing,
    Pussy can climb a tree,
Or play with a silly old cork and string
    To 'muse herself, not me.
But I like *Binkie* my dog, because
    He knows how to behave;
So, *Binkie*'s the same as the First Friend was,
    And I am the Man in the Cave!

Pussy will play Man Friday till
    It's time to wet her paw
And make her walk on the window-sill
    (For the footprint Crusoe saw);
Then she fluffles her tail and mews,
    And scratches and won't attend.
But *Binkie* will play whenever I choose,
    And he is my true First Friend!

Pussy will rub my knees with her head
    Pretending she loves me hard;
But the very minute I go to my bed
    Pussy runs out in the yard,
And there she stays till the morning-light;
    So I know it is only pretend;
But *Binkie*, he snores at my feet all night,
    And he is my Firstest Friend!

—*Just So Stories*, Rudyard Kipling

SLEEK ROTUNDITY

His cellar was well stocked with a selection of the best vintages, under his own especial charge. In all its arrangements his house was a model of order and comfort; and the whole establishment partook of the genial physiognomy of the master. From the master and mistress to the cook, and from the cook to the tom cat, there was about the inhabitants of the vicarage a sleek and purring rotundity of face and figure that denoted community of feelings, habits, and diet; each in its kind, of course, for the Doctor had his port, the cook her ale, and the cat his milk, in sufficiently liberal allowance.

—*Gryll Grange,* Thomas Love Peacock

ZULIA

Zulia, my little cat,
I like you, not for this or that,
But just because you seem to be,
My Zulia, made for me.

If Zulia had a soul,
Why should I care to claim control?
But no such needless longings stir
That vivid peace in her.

Zulia, you love, I know,
The amber shawl that suits you so;
And then how could one but be vain
Of such a ring and chain?

You love to dream, and feel
So good, in church, because you kneel;
You love to dream of lovers, ah!
In Toni's gondola.

You little Japanese,
Made to be pleased, and made to please,
So quaint and smiling, and so small
A dainty animal!

You know that life's a game,
And blanks and prizes just the same,
And all we have to do is, play
The game out, day by day.

Zulia, those eyes were meant
But to be sunnily content;
And those small kiss-curls, one by one,
Kissed over, in the sun.

I kiss them now to-night,
Dear, if you knew with what delight,
You must needs know (and God forbid
My Zulia ever did!)

How one may prejudice
The very honey of a kiss,
When women catch, and men may not
   control,
The new disease of soul.

—Arthur Symons

VERSES ON A CAT

A cat in distress,
Nothing more, nor less;
Good Folks, I must faithfully tell ye,
As I am a sinner,
It waits for some dinner
To stuff out its own little belly.

You would not easily guess
All the modes of distress
Which torture the tenants of earth;
And the various evils,
Which like so many devils,
Attend the poor souls from their birth.

Some a living require,
And others desire
An old fellow out of the way;
And which is the best
I leave to be guessed,
For I cannot pretend to say.

One wants society,
Another variety,
Others a tranquil life;
Some want food.
Others, as good,
Only want a wife.

But this poor little cat
Only wanted a rat,
To stuff out its own little maw;
And it were as good
Some people had such food,
To make them hold their jaw.

—Percy Bysshe Shelley

Nicholas Devore III / Photographers Aspen

19

Gerard Lacz / Animals Animals

CATS IN THE CORN

The corn-spirit sometimes takes the form of a cat. Near Kiel children are warned not to go into the corn-fields because 'the Cat sits there.' In the Eisenach Oberland they are told 'the Corn-cat will come and fetch you,' 'the Corn-cat goes in the corn.' In some parts of Silesia at mowing the last corn they say, 'The Cat is caught'; and at threshing, the man who gives that last stroke is called the Cat. In the neighbourhood of Lyons the last sheaf and the harvest-supper are both called the Cat. About Vesoul when they cut the last corn they say, 'We have the Cat by the tail.' At Briançon, in Dauphiné, at the beginning of reaping, a cat is decked out with ribbons, flowers, and ears of corn. It is called the Cat of the ball-skin *(le chat de peau de balle)*. If a reaper is wounded at his work, they make the cat lick the wound. At the close of the reaping the cat is again decked out with ribbons and ears of corn; then they dance and make merry. When the dance is over the girls solemnly strip the cat of its finery. At Grüneberg, in Silesia, the reaper who cuts the last corn goes by the name of the Tom-cat. He is enveloped in rye-stalks and green withes, and is furnished with a long plaited tail. Sometimes as a companion he has a man similarly dressed, who is called the (female) Cat. Their duty is to run after people whom they see and to beat them with a long stick. Near Amiens the expression for finishing the harvest is, 'They are going to kill the Cat'; and when the last corn is cut they kill a cat in the farmyard. At threshing, in some parts of France, a live cat is placed under the last bundle of corn to be threshed, and is struck dead with the flails. Then on Sunday it is roasted and eaten as a holiday dish. In the Vosges Mountains the close of haymaking or harvest is called 'catching the cat,' 'killing the dog,' or more rarely 'catching the hare.' The cat, the dog, or the hare is said to be fat or lean according as the crop is good or bad. The man who cuts the last handful of hay or of wheat is said to catch the cat or the hare or to kill the dog. He is congratulated by his comrades and has the honour of carrying the nosegay or rather the small fir-tree decked with ribbons which marks the end of the haymaking or of the harvest. In Franche-Comté also the close of harvest is called 'catching or killing the cat.'

—*Spirits of the Corn and of the Wild,* J. G. Frazer

ON A FAVOURITE CAT DROWNED IN A TUB OF GOLDFISHES

Nicholas Devore III / Photographers Aspen

'Twas on a lofty vase's side,
Where China's gayest art had dyed
　　The azure flowers that blow:
Demurest of the tabby kind,
The pensive Selima reclined,
　　Gazed on the lake below.

Her conscious tail her joy declared:
The fair round face, the snowy beard,
　　The velvet of her paws,
Her coat, that with the tortoise vies,
Her ears of jet, and emerald eyes,
　　She saw: and purred applause.

Still had she gazed, but 'midst the tide
Two angel forms were seen to glide,
　　The Genii of the stream:
Their scaly armour's Tyrian hue
Though richest purple to the view
　　Betrayed a golden gleam.

The hapless Nymph with wonder saw:
A whisker first and then a claw,
　　With many an ardent wish,
She stretched in vain to reach the prize.
What female heart can gold despise?
　　What Cat's averse to fish?

Presumptuous Maid! With looks intent
Again she stretched, again she bent,
　　Nor knew the gulf between.
(Malignant Fate sat by and smiled.)
The slippery verge her feet beguiled,
　　She tumbled headlong in.

Eight times emerging from the flood
She mewed to ev'ry wat'ry god
　　Some speedy aid to send.
No Dolphin came, no Nereid stirred:
Nor cruel Tom nor Susan heard—
　　A fav'rite has no friend!

From hence, ye Beauties, undeceived,
Know one false step is ne'er retrieved.
　　And be with caution bold.
Not all that tempts your wand'ring eyes
And heedless hearts, is lawful prize,
　　Nor all that glistens, gold.

—Thomas Gray

21

THE CAT'S PILGRIMAGE

The Cat set off by herself to learn how to be happy, and to be all that a cat could be. It was a fine sunny morning. She determined to try the meadow first, and, after an hour or two, if she had not succeeded, then to go off to the wood. A Blackbird was piping away on a thornbush as if his heart was running over with happiness. The Cat had breakfasted, and so was able to listen without any mixture of feeling. She didn't sneak. She walked boldly up under the bush, and the bird, seeing she had no bad purpose, sat still and sung on.

"Good morning, Blackbird; you seem to be enjoying yourself this fine day."

"Good morning, Cat."

"Blackbird, it is an odd question, perhaps. What ought one to do to be as happy as you?"

"Do your duty, Cat."

"But what is my duty, Blackbird?"

"Take care of your little ones, Cat."

"I haven't any," said she.

"Then sing to your mate," said the bird.

"Tom is dead," said she.

"Poor Cat!" said the bird. "Then sing over his grave. If your song is sad, you will find your heart grow lighter for it."

"Mercy!" thought the Cat. "I could do a little singing with a living lover, but I never heard of singing for a dead one. But you see, bird, it isn't cats' nature. When I am cross, I mew. When I am pleased, I purr; but I must be pleased first. I can't purr myself into happiness."

"I am afraid there is something the matter with your heart, my Cat. It wants warming; good-by."

The Blackbird flew away. The Cat looked sadly after him. "He thinks I am like him; and he doesn't know that a cat is a cat," said she.

—James Anthony Froude

Nicholas Devore III / Photographers Aspen

A MATRIMONIAL THOUGHT

In the blithe days of honeymoon,
   With Kate's allurements smitten,
I lov'd her late, I lov'd her soon,
   And call'd her dearest kitten.

But now my kitten's grown a cat,
   And cross like other wives,
O! by my soul, my honest Mat,
   I fear she has nine lives.

—James Boswell

TO A CAT

Stately, kindly, lordly friend,
    Condescend
Here to sit by me, and turn
Glorious eyes that smile and burn,
Golden eyes, love's lustrous meed,
On the golden page I read.

All your wondrous wealth of hair,
    Dark and fair,
Silken-shaggy, soft and bright
As the clouds and beams of night,
Pays my reverent hand's caress
Back with friendlier gentleness.

Dogs may fawn on all and some,
    As they come;
You, a friend of loftier mind,
Answer friends along in kind;
Just your foot upon my hand
Softly bids it understand.

Wild on woodland ways, your sires
    Flashed like fires;
Fair as flame, and fierce, and fleet,
As with wings on wingless feet,

Shone and sprang your mother, free,
Bright and brave as wind or sea.

Free, and proud, and glad as they,
    Here to-day
Rests or roams their radiant child,
Vanquished not, but reconciled;
Free from curb of aught above
Save the lovely curb of love.

Love, through dreams of souls divine,
    Fain would shine
Round a dawn whose light and song
Then should right our mutual wrong,—
Speak, and seal the love-lit law,
Sweet Assisi's seer foresaw.

Dreams were theirs; yet haply may
    Dawn a day
When such friends and fellows born,
Seeing our earth as fair at morn,
May, for wiser love's sake, see
More of heaven's deep heart than we.

—Algernon Charles Swinburne

'OF FOOD WHICH HAS BEEN ALIVE'

The rat was being besieged in its little dwelling by the weasel which with continual vigilance was awaiting its destruction, and through a tiny chink was considering its great danger. Meanwhile the cat came and suddenly seized hold of the weasel and forthwith devoured it. Whereupon the rat, profoundly grateful to its deity, having offered up some of its hazel-nuts in sacrifice to Jove, came out of its hole in order to repossess itself of the lately lost liberty, and was instantly deprived of this and of life by the cruel claws and teeth of the cat.

—*The Notebooks of Leonardo da Vinci*

THE PAIN-KILLER

Aunt Polly procures a remedy for Tom Sawyer and Tom finds a taker for his aunt's revolting medicine.

Now she heard of Pain-killer for the first time. She ordered a lot at once. She tasted it and was filled with gratitude. It was simply fire in a liquid form. She dropped the water treatment and everything else, and pinned her faith to Pain-killer. She gave Tom

Reneé Stockdale / Animals Animals

a teaspoonful and watched with the deepest anxiety for the result. Her troubles were instantly at rest, her soul at peace again; for the 'indifference' was broken up. The boy could not have shown a wilder, heartier interest if she had built a fire under him.

Tom felt that it was time to wake up; this sort of life might be romantic enough, in his blighted condition but it was getting to have too little sentiment and too much distracting variety about it. So he thought over various plans for relief, and finally hit upon that of professing to be fond of Pain-killer. He asked for it so often that he became a nuisance, and his aunt ended by telling him to help himself and quit bothering her. If it had been Sid, she would have had no misgivings to alloy her delight; but since it was Tom, she watched the bottle clandestinely. She found that the medicine did really diminish, but it did not occur to her that the boy was mending the health of a crack in the sitting-room floor with it.

One day Tom was in the act of dosing the crack when his aunt's yellow cat came along, purring, eying the teaspoon avariciously, and begging for a taste. Tom said:

'Don't ask for it unless you want it, Peter.'

But Peter signified that he did want it.

'You better make sure.'

Peter was sure.

'Now you've asked for it, and I'll give it to you, because there ain't anything mean about *me,* but if you find you don't like it, you mustn't blame anybody but your own self.'

Peter was agreeable. So Tom pried his mouth open and poured down the Pain-killer. Peter sprang a couple of yards in the air, and then delivered a war-whoop and set off round and round the room, banging against furniture, upsetting flower-pots, and making general havoc. Next he rose on his hind feet and pranced around, in a frenzy of enjoyment, with his head over his shoulder and his voice proclaiming his unappeasable happiness. Then he went tearing around the house again spreading chaos and destruction in his path. Aunt Polly entered the room in time to see him throw a few double somersets, deliver a final mighty hurrah, and sail through the open window, carrying him 'thout any more feeling than if he was a human!

Aunt Polly felt a sudden pang of remorse. This was putting the thing in a new light; what was cruelty to a cat *might* be cruelty to a boy, too. She began to soften; she felt sorry. Her eyes watered a little, and she put her hand on Tom's head and said gently:

'I was meaning for the best, Tom. And Tom, it *did* do you good.'

Tom looked up in her face with just a perceptible twinkle peeping through his gravity:

'I know you was meaning for the best, auntie, and so was I with Peter. It done *him* good, too. I never see him get around so since—'

—*The Adventures of Tom Sawyer,* Mark Twain

VENUS AND THE CAT

In ancient times there lived a beautiful cat who fell in love with a young man. Naturally, the young man did not return the cat's affections, so she besought Venus, the goddess of love and beauty, for help. The goddess, taking compassion on her plight, changed her into a fair damsel.

No sooner had the young man set eyes on the maiden than he became enamored of her beauty and in due time led her home as his bride. One evening a short time later, as the young couple were sitting in their chamber, the notion came to Venus to discover whether in changing the cat's form she had also changed her nature. So she set down a mouse before the beautiful damsel. The girl, reverting completely to her former character, started from her seat and pounced upon the mouse as if she would eat it on the spot, while her husband watched her in dismay.

The goddess, provoked by such clear evidence that the girl had revealed her true nature, turned her into a cat again.

Application: WHAT IS BRED IN THE BONE WILL NEVER BE ABSENT IN THE FLESH.

—Aesop

Barbara J. Wright / Animals Animals

'TOBERMORY'

'And do you really ask us to believe,' Sir Wilfrid was saying, 'that you have discovered a means for instructing animals in the art of human speech, and that dear old Tobermory has proved your first successful pupil?'

'It is a problem at which I have worked for the last seventeen years,' said Mr. Appin, 'but only during the last eight or nine months have I been rewarded with glimmerings of success. Of course I have experimented with thousands of animals, but latterly only with cats, those wonderful creatures which have assimilated themselves so marvellously with our civilization while retaining all their highly developed feral instincts. Here and there among cats one comes across an outstanding superior intellect, just as one does among the ruck of human beings, and when I made the acquaintance of Tobermory a week ago I saw at once that I was in contact with a "Beyond-cat" of extraordinary intelligence. I had gone far along the road to success in recent experiments; with Tobermory, as you call him, I have reached the goal.'

Mr. Appin concluded his remarkable statement in a voice which he strove to divest of a triumphant inflection. No one said 'Rats,' though Clovis's lips moved in a monosyllabic contortion which probably invoked those rodents of disbelief.

'And do you mean to say,' asked Miss Resker, after a slight pause, 'that you have taught Tobermory to say and understand easy sentences of one syllable?'

'My dear Miss Resker,' said the wonder-worker patiently, 'one teaches little children and savages and backward adults in that piecemeal fashion; when one has once solved the problem of making a beginning with an animal of highly developed intelligence one has no need for those halting methods. Tobermory can speak our language with perfect correctness.'

This time Clovis very distinctly said, 'beyond-rats!' Sir Wilfrid was more polite, but equally sceptical.

'Hadn't we better have the cat in and judge for ourselves?' suggested Lady Blemley.

Sir Wilfrid went in search of the animal, and the company settled themselves down to the languid expectation of witnessing some more or less adroit drawing-room ventriloquism.

In a minute Sir Wilfrid was back in the room, his face white beneath its tan and his eyes dilated with excitement.

'By Gad, it's true!'

His agitation was unmistakably genuine, and his hearers started forward in a thrill of awakened interest.

Collapsing into an armchair he continued breathlessly: 'I found him dozing in the smoking-room, and called out to him to come for his tea. He blinked at me in his usual way, and I said, "Come on, Toby; don't keep us waiting"; and, by Gad! he drawled out in a most horribly natural voice that he'd come when he dashed well pleased! I nearly jumped out of my skin!'

—*The Chronicles of Clovis,* Saki

Alfred B. Thomas / Animals Animals

TO MRS. REYNOLDS' CAT

Cat! who hast pass'd thy grand climacteric,
  How many mice and rats hast in thy days
  Destroy'd? How many tit bits stolen?
  Gaze
With those bright languid segments green, and prick
Those velvet ears — but pr'ythee do not stick
  Thy latent talons in me — and upraise
  Thy gentle mew — and tell me all thy frays,
Of fish and mice, and rats and tender chick.
Nay, look not down, nor lick thy dainty wrists—
  For all thy wheezy asthma — and for all
Thy tail's tip is nick'd off — and thought the fists
  Of many a maid have given thee many a maul,
Still is that fur as soft, as when the lists
  In youth thou enter'dest on glass bottled wall.
                              —John Keats

Reed / Williams / Animals Animals

THE SPHINX

In a dim corner of my room for longer than my fancy thinks
A beautiful and silent Sphinx has watched me through the
    shifting gloom.

Inviolate and immobile she does not rise she does not stir
For silver moons are naught to her and naught to her the suns that reel.

Red follows grey across the air, the waves of moonlight ebb and flow
But with the Dawn she does not go and in the night-time she is there.

Dawn follows Dawn and Nights grow old and all the while this
    curious cat
Lies couching on the Chinese mat with eyes of satin rimmed
    with gold.

Upon the mat she lies and leers and on the tawny throat of her
Flutters the soft and silky fur or ripples to her pointed ears.

Come forth, my lovely seneschal! so somnolent, so statuesque!
Come forth you exquisite grotesque! half woman and half animal!

Come forth my lovely languorous Sphinx! and put your head upon
    my knee!
And let me stroke your throat and see your body spotted like the Lynx!

And let me touch those curving claws of yellow ivory and grasp
The tail that like a monstrous Asp coils round your heavy velvet paws!

—Oscar Wilde

Nicholas Devore III / Photographers Aspen

THE MYSTERY OF 'THE ZOMBI'

You were duly apprised towards the end of the year of Othello's death. Since that lamented event this house was cat-less, till on Saturday, March 24, Mrs. Calvert, knowing how grievously we were annoyed by rats, offered me what she described as a fine full-grown black cat, who was, moreover, a tom. She gave him an excellent character in all points but one, which was that he was a most expert pigeon-catcher; and as they had a pigeon-house, this propensity rendered it necessary to pass sentence upon him either of transportation or of death. Moved by compassion (his colour and his tomship also being taken into consideration), I consented to give him an asylum, and on the evening of that day here he came in a sack.

You, Grosvenor, who are a *philogalist,* and therefore understand more of cat nature than has been ever attained by the most profound naturalists, know how difficult it is to reconcile a cat to a new domicile. When the sack was opened, the kitchen door, which leads into the passage, was open also, and the cat disappeared; not indeed like a flash of lightning, but as fast as one—that is to say, for all purposes or a simile. There was no chance of his making his way back to the pigeon-house. He might have done this had he been carried thrice the distance in any other direction; but in this there was either a river to cross, or a part of the town to pass, both of which were such obstacles to his travels that we were quite sure all on this side of them was to him *terra incognita.* Food, therefore, was placed where he would be likely to find it in the night; and at the unanimous desire of the children, I took upon myself the charge of providing him with a name, for it is not proper that a cat should remain without one. Taking into consideration his complexion, as well as his sex, my first thought was to call him Henrique Diaz, a name which poor Koster would have approved, had he been living to have heard it; but it presently occurred to me that The Zombi would be an appellation equally appropriate and more dignified. The Zombi, therefore, he was named.

It was soon ascertained that The Zombi had taken possession of poor Wilsey's cellar, which being filled with pea-sticks afforded him a secure hiding-place; the kitchen also of that part of the house being forsaken, he was in perfect quiet. Food was laid for him every day, and the children waited impatiently for the time when The Zombi would become acquainted with the house, and suffer them to become acquainted with him. Once or twice in the evening he was seen out of doors, and it was known that he reconnoitred the premises in the night; but in obstinate retirement he continued from Saturday till Saturday, seven days and nights, notwithstanding all kind words were used to bring him out, as if he had been determined to live and die a hermit.

But between four and five o'clock on the Sunday morning, all who had ears to hear were awakened by such screams as if The Zombi had been caught in a rat-trap, or had met with some other excruciating accident. You, Mr. Bedford, understand cats, and know very well that a cat-*solo* is a very different thing from a *duet*; and that no person versed in their tongue can mistake their expression of pain for anything else.

The creature seemed to be in agonies. A light was procured, that it might be relieved if that were possible. Upon searching the house, The Zombi was seen at the top of Wilsey's stairs, from whence he disappeared, retreating to his stronghold in the cellar; nor could any traces be discovered of any hurt that could have befallen him, nor has it since appeared that he had received any, so that the cause of this nocturnal disturbance remains an impenetrable mystery.

Various have been our attempts to explain it. Some of the women who measure the power of rats by their own fears, would have it that he was bitten by a rat, or by an association of rats; but to this I indignantly replied that in that case the ground would have been strewn with their bodies, and that it would have been the rats' cry, not The Zombi's, that would have been heard. Dismissing, therefore, that impossible supposition, I submit to your consideration, in the form of queries, the various possibilities which have occurred to me—all unsatisfactory, I confess—requesting you to assist me in my endeavour to find out the mystery of this wonderful history, as it may truly be called. You will be pleased to bear in mind that The Zombi was the only cat concerned in the transaction: of that I am perfectly certain.

Now then, Grosvenor—
1. Had he seen the devil?
2. Was he making love to himself?
3. Was he engaged in single combat with himself?
4. Was he attempting to raise the devil by invocation?
5. Had he heard me sing, and was he attempting (vainly) to imitate it?

These queries, you will perceive, all proceed upon the supposition that it was The Zombi who made the noise. But I have further to ask—
6. Was it the devil?
7. Was it Jeffery?★
8. Were either of these personages tormenting The Zombi?

I have only to add that from that time to this he continues in the same obstinate retirement, and to assure you that
> I remain,
> Mr. Bedford,
> > With the highest consideration,
> > > Yours as ever,
> > > Robert Southey

P.S.—One further query occurs while I am writing. Sunday having been the first of the month—
9. Was he making April fools of us?

—Robert Southey

31

THE DOG AND THE CAT

They both of them sit by my fire every Evening and wait with Impatience; and at my Entrance, never fail of running up to me, and bidding me Welcome, each of them in its proper Language. As they have been bred up together from Infancy, and have seen no other Company, they have acquired each other's Manners; so that the Dog gives himself the Airs of a Cat, and the Cat, in several of her Motions and Gestures, affects the Behaviour of the little Dog.

—Richard Steele

THE KITTEN

Wanton droll, whose harmless play
Beguiles the rustic's closing day,
When, drawn the evening fire about,
Sit aged crone and thoughtless lout,
And child upon his three-foot stool,
Waiting until his supper cool,
And maid, whose cheek outblooms the rose,
As bright the blazing fagot glows,
Who, bending to the friendly light,
Plies her task with busy sleight;
Come, show thy tricks and sportive graces,
Thus circled round with merry faces!

Backward coil'd and crouching low,
With glaring eyeballs watch thy foe,
The housewife's spindle whirling round,
Or thread or straw that on the ground
Its shadow throws, by urchin sly
Held out to lure thy roving eye;
Then stealing onward, fiercely spring
Upon the tempting faithless thing.
Now, wheeling round with bootless skill,
Thy bo-peep tail provokes thee still,
As still beyond thy curving side
Its jetty tip is seen to glide;
Till from thy centre starting far,
Thou sidelong veerst with rump in air
Erected stiff, and gait awry,
Like madam in her tantrums high;
Though ne'er a madam of them all,
Whose silken kirtle sweeps the hall,
More varied trick and whim displays
To catch the admiring stranger's gaze.

Doth power in measured verses dwell,
All thy vagaries wild to tell?
Ah no! the start, the jet, the bound,
The giddy scamper round and round,
With leap and toss and high curvet,
And many a whirling somerset,
(Permitted by the modern muse
Expression technical to use)
These mock the deftest rhymester's skill,
But poor in art, though rich in will.

The featest tumbler, stage bedight,
To thee is but a clumsy wight,
Who every limb and sinew strains
To do what costs thee little pains;
For which, I trow, the gaping crowd
Require him oft with plaudits loud.

But, stopp'd the while thy wanton play,
Applauses too thy pains repay:
For then, beneath some urchin's hand
With modest pride thou tak'st thy stand,
While many a stroke of kindness glides

Along thy back and tabby sides.
Dilated swells thy glossy fur,
And loudly croons thy busy purr,
As, timing well the equal sound,
Thy clutching feet bepat the ground,
And all their harmless claws disclose
Like prickles of an early rose,
While softly from thy whisker'd cheek
Thy half-closed eyes peer, mild and meek.

But not alone by cottage fire
Do rustics rude thy feats admire.
The learned sage, whose thoughts explore
The widest range of human lore,
Or with unfetter'd fancy fly
Through airy heights of poesy,
Pausing smiles with alter'd air
To see thee climb his elbow-chair,
Or, struggling on the mat below,
Hold warfare with his slipper'd toe.
The widow'd dame or lonely maid,
Who, in the still but cheerless shade
Of home unsocial, spends her age,
And rarely turns a letter'd page,
Upon her hearth for thee lets fall
The rounded cork or paper ball,
Nor chides thee on thy wicked watch,
The ends of ravell'd skein to catch,
But lets thee have thy wayward will,
Perplexing oft her better skill.

E'en he, whose mind of gloomy bent,
In lonely tower or prison pent,
Reviews the coil of former days,
And loathes the world and all its ways.
What time the lamp's unsteady gleam
Hath roused him from his moody dream,
Feels, as thou gambol'st round his seat,
His heart of pride less fiercely beat,
And smiles, a link in thee to find,
That joins it still to living kind.

Whence hast thou then, thou witless puss!
The magic power to charm us thus?
Is it that in thy glaring eye
And rapid movements, we descry –
Whilst we at ease, secure from ill,
The chimney corner snugly fill –
A lion darting on his prey,
A tiger at his ruthless play?
Or is it that in thee we trace,
With all thy varied wanton grace,
An emblem, view'd with kindred eye,
Of tricky, restless infancy?
Ah! many a lightly sportive child,
Who hath like thee our wits beguiled,
To dull and sober manhood grown,
With strange recoil our hearts disown.

Nicholas Devore III / Photographers Aspen

And so, poor kit! must thou endure,
When thou becom'st a cat demure,
Full many a cuff and angry word,
Chased roughly from the tempting board.
But yet, for that thou hast, I ween,
So oft our favour'd play-mate been,
Soft be the change which thou shalt prove!
When time hath spoil'd thee of our love,
Still be thou deem'd by housewife fat
A comely, careful, mousing cat,
Whose dish is, for the public good,
Replenish'd oft with savoury food,
Nor, when thy span of life is past,
Be thou to pond or dung-hill cast,
But, gently borne on goodman's spade,
Beneath the decent sod be laid;
And children show with glistening eyes
The place where poor old pussy lies.

—*Dramatic and Poetical Works,* Joanna Baillie

Henry Ausloos / Animals Animals

'FOR WHO WOLDE SENGE
A CATTES SKYN'

For who wolde senge a cattes skyn,
Thanne wolde the cat wel dwellen in his in;
And if the cattes skyn be slyk and gay,
She wol nat dwelle in house half a day;
But forth she wole, er any day be dawed,
To shewe hir skyn, and goon a-catterwawed.
                    —Geoffrey Chaucer

ST. JEROME AND HIS LION

St. Jerome in his study kept a great big cat,
It's always in his pictures, with its feet upon the mat.
Did he give it milk to drink, in a little dish?
When it came to Fridays, did he give it fish?
If I lost my little cat, I'd be sad without it;
I should ask St. Jeremy what to do about it;
I should ask St. Jeremy, just because of that,
For he's the only saint I know who kept a pussy cat.
                    —Anonymous

Nicholas Devore III / Photographers Aspen

THE OLD WOMAN AND HER CATS

A wrinkled hag, of wicked fame,
Beside a little smoky flame
Sat hovering, pinched with age and frost;
Her shrivelled hands, with veins embossed,
Upon her knees her weight sustain,
While palsy shook her crazy brains;
She mumbles forth her backward prayers,
An untamed scold of fourscore years.
About her swarmed a numerous brood
Of Cats, who lank with hunger mewed.
Teased with their cries her choler grew,
And thus she sputtered, "Hence, ye crew!
Fool that I was, to entertain
Such imps, such fiends, a hellish train!
Had ye been never housed and nursed,
I for a witch had ne'er been cursed.
To you I owe, that crowds of boys
Worry me with eternal noise;

Straws laid across my pace retard,
The horse-shoe's nailed (each threshold's guard).
The stunted broom the wenches hide,
For fear that I should up and ride".

. . . .

"To hear you prate would vex a saint;
Who hath most reason of complaint?"
Replies a Cat. "Let's come to proof.
Had we ne'er starved beneath your roof,
We had, like others of our race,
In credit lived, as beasts of chase.
'Tis infamy to serve a hag;
Cats are thought imps, her broom a nag;
And boys against our lives combine,
Because, 'tis said, your cats have nine".

—John Gay

Robert Maier / Animals Animals

THE KITTEN ON THE WALL

See the Kitten on the wall,
Sporting with the leaves that fall,
Withered leaves — one — two — and three —
From the lofty elder-tree
. . . .
But the kitten, how she starts,
Crouches, stretches, paws, and darts
First at one, and then its fellow,
Just as light and just as yellow;
There are many now — now one—
Now they stop and there are none:
What intenseness of desire
In her upward eye of fire
With a tiger-leap half-way
Now she meets the coming prey,
Lets it go as fast, and then
Has it in her power again:
Now she works with three or four,
Like an Indian conjuror;
Quick as he in feats of art,
Far beyond in joy of heart.
Were her antics played in the eye
Of a thousand standers-by,
Clapping hands with shout and stare,
What would little Tabby care
For the plaudits of the crowd?
Over happy to be proud,
Over wealthy in the treasure
Of her own exceeding pleasure.

—William Wordsworth

ON THE DEATH OF A CAT

Who shall tell the lady's grief
When her Cat was past relief?
Who shall number the hot tears
Shed o'er her, belov'd for years?
Who shall say the dark dismay
Which her dying caused that day?

Come, ye Muses, one and all,
Come obedient to my call;
Come and mourn with tuneful breath
Each one for a separate death;
And, while you in numbers sigh,
I will sing her elegy.

Of a noble race she came,
And Grimalkin was her name.
Young and old fully many a mouse
Felt the prowess of her house;

Weak and strong fully many a rat
Cowered beneath her crushing pat;
And the birds around the place
Shrank from her too close embrace.

But one night, reft of her strength,
She lay down and died at length;
Lay a kitten by her side
In whose life the mother died.
Spare her line and lineage,
Guard her kitten's tender age,
And that kitten's name as wide
Shall be known as hers that died.
And whoever passes by
The poor grave where Puss doth lie,
Softly, softly let him tread,
Nor disturb her narrow bed.
—Christina Rossetti

Nicholas Devore III / Photographers Aspen

THE MASION

This beaste is called a 'Masion', for that he is enimie to Myse and Rattes. He is slye and wittie, and seeth so sharpely that he over-commeth darkness of the nighte by the shyninge lyghte of his eyne. In shape of body he is like unto a Leoparde, and hathe a great mouthe. He doth delighte that he enjoyeth his libertie; and in his youth he is swifte, plyante, and merye. He maketh a rufull noyse and a gastefull when he profereth to fighte with another. He is a cruell beaste when he is wilde, and falleth on his owne feete from moste highe places: and never is hurt therewith. When he hathe a fayre skinne, he is, as it were, proude thereof, and then he goethe muche aboute to be seene.

—*Workes of Armorie,* John Bossewell

THE REMARKABLEST CAT

One of my comrades there [at a Californian mining camp] – another of those victims of eighteen years of unrequited toil and blighted hopes – was one of the gentlest spirits that ever bore its patient cross in a weary exile: grave and simple Dick Baker, pocket miner of Dead-House Gulch. He was forty-six, grey as a rat, earnest, thoughtful, slenderly educated, slouchily dressed and clay-soiled, but his heart was finer metal than ever was mined or minted.

Whenever he was out of luck and a little down-hearted, he would fall to mourning over the loss of a wonderful cat he used to own (for where women and children are not, men of kindly impulses take up with pets, for they must love something). And he always spoke of the strange sagacity of that cat with the air of a man who believed in his secret heart that there was something human about it – maybe even supernatural.

I heard him talking about this animal once. He said:

'Gentlemen, I used to have a cat here, by the name of Tom Quartz, which you'd took an interest in, I reckon – most anybody would. I had him here eight year – and he was the remarkablest cat *I* ever see. He was a large grey one of the Tom specie, an' he had more hard, natchral sense than any man in this camp – 'n' a *power* of dignity – he wouldn't let the Guv'nor of Californy be familiar with him. He never ketched a rat in his life – 'peared to be above it. He never cared for nothing but mining. He knowed more about mining, that cat did, than any man *I* ever, ever see. You couldn't tell *him* noth'n' 'bout placer diggin's – 'n' as for pocket mining, why, he was just born for it. He would dig out after man an' Jim when we went over the hills prospect'n', and he would trot along behind us for as much as five mile, if we went so fur. An' he had the best judgment about mining ground – why, you never see anything like it. When we went to work, he'd scatter a glance around, 'n' if he didn't think much of the indications, he would give a look as much as to say, 'Well, I'll have to get you to excuse *me*'; 'n' without another word he'd hyste his nose into the air 'n' shove for home. But if the ground suited him, he would lay low 'n' keep dark till the first pan was washed, 'n' then he would sidle up 'n' take a look, and' if there was about six or seven grains of gold *he* was satisfied – he didn't want no better prospect n' that – 'n' then he would lay down on our coats and snore like a steamboat till we'd struck the pocket, an' then get up 'n' superintend. He was nearly lightnin' on superintending.

'Well, by-an'-bye, up comes this yer quartz excitement. Everybody was into it – everybody was pick'n' 'n' blast'n' instead of shovellin' dirt on the hill-side – everybody was put'n' down a shaft instead of scrapin' the surface. Noth'n' would do Jim but *we* must tackle the ledges, too, 'n' so we did. We commenced put'n' down a shaft, 'n' Tom Quartz he begin to wonder what in the Dickens it was all about. *He* hadn't ever seen any mining like that before, 'n' he was all upset, as you may say – he couldn't come to a right understanding of it no way– it was too many for *him*. He was down on it, too, you bet you – he was down on it powerful – 'n' always appeared to consider it the cussedest foolishness out. But that cat, you know, was *always* agin new-fangled arrangements – somehow he never could abide 'em. *You* know how it is with old habits. But by-an'-bye Tom Quartz begin to git sort of reconciled a little, though he never *could* altogether understand that eternal sinkin' of a shaft an' never pannin' out anything. At last he got to comin' down in the shaft, his-self, to try to cipher it out. An' when he'd git the blues, 'n' feel kind of scruffy, 'n' aggravated 'n' disgusted – knowin', as he did, that the bills was runnin' up all the time an' we warn't makin' a cent

Nicholas Devore III / Photographers Aspen

– he would curl up on a gunny-sack in the corner an' go to sleep. Well, one day when the shaft was down about eight foot, the rock got so hard that we had to put in a blast – the first blast'n' we'd ever done since Tom Quartz was born. An' then we lit the fuse, 'n' clumb out 'n' got off 'bout fifty yards – 'n' forgot 'n' left Tom Quartz sound asleep on the gunny-sack. In 'bout a minute we seen a puff of smoke bust up out of the hole, 'n' then everything let go with an awful crash, 'n' about four million ton of rocks 'n' dirt 'n' smoke 'n' splinters shot up 'bout a mile an' a half into the air, an' by George, right in the dead centre of it was old Tom Quartz a-goin' end over end, an' a snortin' an' a sneez'n', an' a clawin' an' a reachin' for things like all possessed. But it warn't no use, you know, it warn't no use. An' that was the last we see of *him* for about two minutes 'n' a half, an' then all of a sudden it begin to rain rocks and rubbage, an' directly he come down kerwhop about ten foot off f'm where we stood. Well, I reckon he was p'raps the orneriest-lookin' beast you ever see. One ear was sot back on his neck, 'n' his tail was stove up, 'n' his eye-winkers was swinged off, 'n' he was all blacked up with powder an' smoke, an' all sloppy with mud 'n' slush f'm one end to the other. Well, sir, it arn't no use to try to apologize – we couldn't say a word. He took a sort of a disgusted look at hisself, 'n' then he looked at us – an' it was just exactly the same as if he had said – "Gents, maybe *you* think it's smart to take advantage of a cat that 'ain't had no experience of quartz minin', but *I* think *different*" – an' then he turned on his heel 'n' marched off home without ever saying another word.

'That was jest his style. An' maybe you won't believe it, but after that you never see a cat so prejudiced agin quartz mining as what he was. An' by-an'-bye when he *did* get to goin' down in the shaft again, you'd 'a been astonished at his sagacity. The minute we'd tetch off a blast 'n' the fuse'd begin to sizzle, he'd give a look as much to say, "Well, I'll have to git you to excuse *me*," an' it was surpris'n' the way he'd shin out of that hole 'n' go f'r a tree. Sagacity? It ain't no name for it. 'Twas *inspiration!*'

I said, 'Well, Mr. Baker, his prejudice against quartz mining *was* remarkable, considering how he came by it. Couldn't you ever cure him of it?'

'*Cure him!* No! When Tom Quartz was sot once, he was *always* sot – and you might a blowed him up as much as three million times 'n' you'd never a broken him of his cussed prejudice agin quartz mining.'

The affection and the pride that lit up Baker's face when he delivered this tribute to the firmness of his humble friend of other days will always be a vivid memory with me.

—*The Innocents At Home*, Mark Twain

THE VAMPIRE CAT OF NABÉSHIMA

There is a tradition in the Nabéshima family that, many years ago, the Prince of Hizen was bewitched and cursed by a cat that had been kept by one of his retainers. This prince had in his house a lady of rare beauty, called O Toyo: amongst all his ladies she was the favourite, and there was none who could rival her charms and accomplishments. One day the Prince went out into the garden with O Toyo, and remained enjoying the fragrance of the flowers until sunset, when they returned to the palace, never noticing that they were being followed by a large cat. Having parted with her lord, O Toyo retired to her own room and went to bed. At midnight she awoke with a start, and became aware of a huge cat that crouched watching her; and when she cried out, the beast sprang on her, and, fixing its cruel teeth in her delicate throat, throttled her to death. What a piteous end for so fair a dame, the darling of her prince's heart, to die suddenly, bitten to death by a cat! Then the cat, having scratched out a grave under the verandah, buried the corpse of O Toyo, and assuming her form, began to bewitch the Prince.

But my lord the Prince knew nothing of all this, and little thought that the beautiful creature who caressed and fondled him was an impish and foul beast that had slain his mistress and assumed her shape in order to drain out his life's blood. Day by day, as time went on, the Prince's strength dwindled away; the colour of his face was changed, and became pale and livid; and he was as a man suffering from a deadly sickness. Seeing this, his councillors and his wife became greatly alarmed; so they summoned the physicians, who prescribed various remedies for him; but the more medicine he took, the more serious did his illness appear, and no treatment was of any avail. But most of all did he suffer in the night-time, when his sleep would be troubled and disturbed by hideous dreams. In consequence of this, his councillors nightly appointed a hundred of his retainers to sit up and watch over him; but, strange to say, towards ten o'clock on the very first night that the watch was set, the guard were seized with a sudden and unaccountable drowsiness, which they could not resist, until one by one every man had fallen asleep. Then the false O Toyo came in and harassed the Prince until morning. The following night the same thing occurred, and the Prince was subjected to the imp's tyranny, while his guards slept helplessly around him. Night after night this was repeated, until at last three of the Prince's councillors determined themselves to sit up on guard, and see whether they could overcome this mysterious drowsiness; but they fared no better than the others, and by ten o'clock were fast asleep. The next day the three councillors held a solemn conclave, and their chief, one Isahaya Buzen, said –

'This is a marvellous thing, that a guard of a hundred men should thus be overcome by sleep. Of a surety, the spell that is upon my lord and upon his guard must be the work of witchcraft. Now, as all our efforts are of no avail, let us seek out Ruiten, the chief priest of the temple called Miyó In, and beseech him to put up prayers for the recovery of my lord.'

And the other councillors approving what Isahaya Buzen had said, they went to the priest Ruiten and engaged him to recite litanies that the Prince might be restored to health.

So it came to pass that Ruiten, the chief priest of Miyó In, offered up prayers nightly for the Prince. One night, at the ninth hour (midnight), when he had finished his religious exercises and was preparing to lie down to sleep, he fancied that he heard a noise outside in the garden, as if some one were washing himself at the well. Deeming this passing strange, he looked down from the window; and there in the moonlight he saw a handsome young soldier, some twenty-four years of age, washing himself, who, when he had finished cleaning himself and had put on his clothes, stood before the figure of Buddha and prayed fervently for the recovery of my lord the Prince. Ruiten looked on with admiration; and the young man, when he had made an end of his prayer, was going away; but the priest stopped him, calling out to him –

'Sir, I pray you to tarry a little: I have something to say to you.'

'At your reverence's service. What may you please to want?'

'Pray be so good as to step up here, and have a little talk.'

'By your reverence's leave;' and with this he went upstairs.

Then Ruiten said –

'Sir, I cannot conceal my admiration that you, being so young a man, should have so loyal a spirit. I am Ruiten, the chief priest of this temple, who am engaged in praying for the recovery of my lord. Pray what is your name?'

'My name, sir, is Itô Sôda, and I am serving in the infantry of Nabéshima. Since my lord has been sick, my one desire has been to assist in nursing him; but, being only a simple soldier, I am not of sufficient rank to come into his presence, so I have no resource but to pray to the gods of the country and to Buddha that my lord may regain his health.'

When Ruiten heard this, he shed tears in admiration of the fidelity of Itô Sôda, and said –

'Your purpose is, indeed, a good one; but what a strange sickness this is that my lord is afflicted with! Every night he suffers from horrible dreams; and the retainers who sit up with him are all seized with a mysterious sleep, so that not one can keep awake. It is very wonderful.'

'Yes,' replied Sôda, after a moment's reflection, 'this certainly must be witchcraft. If I could but obtain leave to sit up one night with the Prince, I would fain see whether I could not resist this drowsiness and detect the goblin.'

At last the priest said, 'I am in relations of friendship with Isahaya Buzen, the chief councillor of the Prince. I will speak to him of you and of your loyalty, and will intercede with him that you may attain your wish.'

'Indeed, sir, I am most thankful. I am not prompted by any vain thought of self-advancement, should I succeed: all I wish for is the recovery of my lord. I commend myself to your kind favour.'

'Well, then, to-morrow night I will take you with me to the councillor's house.'

'Thank you, sir, and farewell.' And so they parted.

On the following evening Itô Sôda returned to the temple Miyó In, and having found Ruiten, accompanied him to the house of Isahaya Buzen: then the priest, leaving Sôda outside, went in to converse with the councillor, and inquire after the Prince's health.

'And pray, sir, how is my lord? Is he in any better condition since I have been offering up prayers for him?'

'Indeed, no; his illness is very severe. We are certain that he must be the victim of some foul sorcery; but as there are no means of keeping a guard awake after ten o'clock, we cannot catch a sight of the goblin, so we are in the greatest trouble.'

'I feel deeply for you: it must be most distressing. However, I have something to tell you. I think that I have found a man who will detect the goblin; and I have brought him with me.'

'Indeed! who is the man?'

'Well, he is one of my lord's foot-soldiers, named Itô Sôda, a faithful fellow, and I trust that you will grant his request to be permitted to sit up with my lord.'

'Certainly, it is wonderful to find so much loyalty and zeal in a common soldier,' replied Isahaya Buzen, after a moment's reflection; 'still it is impossible to allow a man of such low rank to perform the office of watching over my lord.'

'It is true that he is but a common soldier,' urged the priest; 'but why not raise his rank in consideration of his fidelity, and then let him mount guard?'

'It would be time enough to promote him after my lord's recovery. But come, let me see this Itô Sôda, that I may know what manner of man he is: if he pleases me, I will consult with the other councillors, and perhaps we may grant him his request.'

'I will bring him in forthwith,' replied Ruiten, who thereupon went out to fetch the young man.

When he returned, the priest presented Itô Sôda to the councillor, who looked at him attentively, and, being pleased with his comely and gentle appearance, said –

'So I hear that you are anxious to be permitted to mount guard in my lord's room at night. Well, I must consult with the other councillors, and we will see what can be done for you.'

When the young soldier heard this he was greatly elated, and took his leave, after warmly thanking Ruiten, who had helped him to gain his object. The next day the councillors held a meeting, and sent for Itô Sôda, and told him that he might keep watch with the other retainers that very night. So he went his way in high spirits, and at nightfall, having made all his preparations, took his place among the hundred gentlemen who were on duty in the prince's bedroom.

Now the Prince slept in the centre of the room, and the hundred guards around him sat keeping themselves awake with entertaining conversation and pleasant conceits. But, as ten o'clock approached, they began to doze off as they sat; and in spite of all their endeavours to keep one another awake, by degrees they all fell asleep. Itô Sôda all this while felt an irresistible desire to sleep creeping over him, and, though he tried by all sorts of ways to rouse himself, he saw that there was no help for it, but by resorting to an extreme measure, for which he had already made his preparations. Drawing out a piece of oil paper which he had brought with him, and spreading it over the mats, he sat down upon it; then he took the small knife which he carried in the sheath of his dirk, and stuck it into his own thigh. For awhile the pain of the wound kept him awake; but as the slumber by which he was assailed was the work of sorcery, little by little he became drowsy again. Then he twisted the knife round and round in his thigh, so that the pain becoming very violent, he was proof against the feeling of sleepiness, and kept a faithful watch. Now the oil paper which he had spread under his leg was in order to prevent the blood, which might spurt from his wound, from defiling the mats.

So Itô Sôda remained awake, but the rest of the guard slept; and as he watched, suddenly the sliding-doors of the Prince's room were drawn open, and he saw a figure coming stealthily, and, as it drew nearer, the form was that of a marvellously beautiful woman some twenty-three years of age. Cautiously she looked around her; and when she saw that all the guard were asleep, she smiled an ominous smile, and was going up to the Prince's bed-side, when she perceived that in one corner of the room there was a man yet awake. This seemed to startle her, but she went up to Sôda and said –

'I am not used to seeing you here. Who are you?'

'My name is Itô Sôda, and this is the first night that I have been on guard.' 'A troublesome office, truly! Why, here are all the rest of the guard asleep. How is it that you alone are awake? You are a trusty watchman.'

'There is nothing to boast about. I'm asleep myself, fast and sound.'

'What is that wound on your knee? It is all red with blood.'

'Oh! I felt very sleepy; so I stuck my knife into my thigh, and the pain of it has kept me awake.'

'What wondrous loyalty!' said the lady.

'Is it not the duty of a retainer to lay down his life for his master? Is such a scratch as this worth thinking about?'

Then the lady went up to the sleeping prince and said, 'How fares it with my lord to-night?' But the Prince, worn out with sickness, made no reply. But Sôda was watching her eagerly, and guessed that it was O Toyo, and made up his mind that if she attempted to harass the Prince he would kill her on the spot. The goblin, however, which in the form of O Toyo had been tormenting the Prince every night, and had come again that night for no other purpose, was defeated by the watchfulness of Itô Sôda; for whenever she drew near to the sick man, thinking to put her spells upon him, she would turn and look behind her, and there she saw Itô Sôda glaring at her; so she had no help for it but to go away again, and leave the Prince undisturbed.

At last the day broke, and the other officers, when they awoke and opened their eyes, saw that Itô Sôda had kept awake by stabbing himself in the thigh; and they were greatly ashamed, and went home crestfallen.

That morning Itô Sôda went to the house of Isahaya Buzen, and told him all that had occurred the previous night. The councillors were all loud in their praise of Itô Sôda's behaviour, and ordered him to keep watch again that night. At the same hour, the false O Toyo came and looked all round the room, and all of the guard were asleep, excepting Itô Sôda, who was wide awake, and so, being again frustrated, she returned to her own apartments.

Now as since Sôda had been on guard the Prince had passed quiet nights, his sickness began to get better, and there was great joy in the palace, and Sôda was promoted and rewarded with an estate. In the meanwhile O Toyo, seeing that her nightly visits bore no fruits, kept away; and from that time forth the night-guard were no longer subject to fits of drowsiness. This coincidence struck Sôda as very strange, so he went to Isahaya Buzen and told him that of a certainty this O Toyo was no other than a goblin. Isahaya Buzen reflected for a while, and said –

'Well, then, how shall we kill the foul thing?'

'I will go to the creature's room, as if nothing were the matter, and try to kill her; but in case she should try to escape, I will beg you to order eight men to stop outside and lie in wait for her.'

Having agreed upon this plan, Sôda went at nightfall to O Toyo's apartment, pretending to have been sent with a message from the Prince. When she saw him arrive, she said –

'What message have you brought me from my lord?'

'Oh! nothing in particular. Be so good as to look at this letter;' and as he spoke, he drew near to her, and suddenly drawing his dirk cut at her; but the goblin, springing back, seized a halberd, and glaring fiercely at Sôda, said –

'How dare you behave like this to one of your lord's ladies? I will have you dismissed;' and she tried to strike Sôda with the halberd. But Sôda fought desperately with his dirk; and the goblin, seeing that she was no match for him, threw away the halberd, and from a beautiful woman became suddenly transformed into a cat, which, springing up the sides of the room, jumped on to the roof. Isahaya Buzen and his eight men who were watching outside shot at the cat, but missed it, and the beast made good its escape.

So the cat fled to the mountains, and did much mischief among the surrounding people, until at last the Prince of Hizen ordered a great hunt, and the beast was killed.

But the Prince recovered from his sickness; and Itô Sôda was richly rewarded.

—*Tales of Old Japan,* Lord Redesdale

Sydney Thomson / Animals Animals

CHARLES DICKENS' CAT

On account of our birds, cats were not allowed in the house; but from a friend in London I received a present of a white kitten – Williamina – and she and her numerous offspring had a happy home at 'Gad's Hill.' She became a favorite with all the household, and showed particular devotion to my father. I remember on one occasion when she had presented us with a family of kittens, she selected a corner of my father's study for their home. She brought them one by one from the kitchen and deposited them in her chosen corner. My father called to me to remove them, saying that he could not allow the kittens to remain in his room. I did so, but Williamina brought them back again, one by one. Again they were removed. The third time, instead of putting them in the corner, she placed them all, and herself beside them, at my father's feet, and gave him such an imploring glance that he could resist no longer, and they were allowed to remain. As the kittens grew older they became more and more frolicsome, swarming up the curtains, playing about on the writing table and scampering behind the book shelves. But they were never complained of and lived happily in the study until the time came for finding them other homes. One of these kittens was kept, who, as he was quite deaf, was left unnamed, and became known by the servants as 'the master's cat,' because of his devotion to my father. He was always with him, and used to follow him about the garden like a dog, and sit with him while he wrote. One evening we were all, except father, going to a ball, and when we started, left 'the master' and his cat in the drawing-room together. 'The master' was reading at a small table, on which a lighted candle was placed. Suddenly the candle went out. My father, who was much interested in his book, relighted the candle, stroked the cat, who was looking at him pathetically he noticed, and continued his reading. A few minutes later, as the light became dim, he looked up just in time to see puss deliberately put out the candle with his paw, and then look appealingly toward him. This second and unmistakable hint was not disregarded, and puss was given the petting he craved. Father was full of this anecdote when all met at breakfast the next morning.

—*My Father As I Recall Him*, Mamie Dickens

THE CAT AND THE FOX

A fox was boasting to a cat one day about how clever he was. "Why, I have a whole bag of tricks," he bragged. "For instance, I know of at least a hundred different ways of escaping my enemies, the dogs."

"How remarkable," said the cat. "As for me, I have only one trick, though I usually make it work. I wish you could teach me some of yours."

"Well, sometime when I have nothing else to do," said the fox, "I might teach you one or two of my easier ones."

Just at that moment they heard the yelping of a pack of hounds. They were coming straight toward the spot where the cat and the fox stood. Like a flash the cat scampered up a tree and disappeared in the foliage. "This is the trick I told you about," she called down to the fox. "It's my only one. Which trick are you going to use?"

The fox sat there trying to decide which of his many tricks he was going to employ. Nearer and nearer came the hounds. When it was quite too late, the fox decided to run for it. But even before he started the dogs were upon him, and that was the end of the fox, bagful of tricks and all!

Application: ONE GOOD PLAN THAT WORKS IS BETTER
THAN A HUNDRED DOUBTFUL ONES.

'LAST WORDS TO A DUMB FRIEND'

Pet was never mourned as you,
Purrer of the spotless hue,
Plumy tail, and wistful gaze,
While you humoured our queer ways,
Or outshrilled your morning call
Up the stairs and through the hall –
Foot suspended in its fall –
While, expectant, you would stand
Arched, to meet the stroking hand;
Till your way you chose to wend
Yonder, to your tragic end.

Never another pet for me!
Let your place all vacant be;
Better blankness day by day
Than companion torn away.
Better bid his memory fade,
Better blot each mark he made,
Selfishly escape distress
By contrived forgetfulness,

Than preserve his prints to make
Every morn and eve an ache.

From the chair whereon he sat
Sweep his fur, nor wince thereat;
Rake his little pathways out
Mid the bushes roundabout;
Smooth away his talons' mark
From the claw-worn pine-tree bark,
Where he climbed as dusk enbrowned
Waiting us who loitered round.

Strange it is this speechless thing,
Subject to our mastering,
Subject for his life and food
To our gift, and time, and mood;
Timid pensioner of us Powers,
His existence ruled by ours,
Should – by crossing at a breath
Into safe and shielded death,
By the merely taking hence

Of his insignificance –
Loom as largened to the sense,
Shape as part, above man's will,
Of the Imperturbable.

As a prisoner, flight debarred,
Exercising in a yard,
Still retain I, troubled, shaken,
Mean estate, by him forsaken;
And this home, which scarcely took
Impress from his little look,
By his faring to the Dim,
Grows all eloquent of him.

Housemate, I can think you still
Bounding to the window-sill,
Over which I vaguely see,
Your small mound beneath the tree,
Showing in the autumn shade
That you moulder where you played.
—Thomas Hardy

SIR JOHN LANGBORN'S TITLES

Jeremy Bentham was very fond of animals, particularly *'pussies,'* as he called them, 'when they had domestic virtues;' but he had no particular affection for the common race of *cats*. He had one, however, of which he used to boast that he had 'made a man of him,' and whom he was wont to invite to eat maccaroni at his own table. This puss got knighted, and rejoiced in the name of Sir John Langborn. In his early days he was a frisky, inconsiderate, and, to say the truth, somewhat profligate gentleman; and had, according to the report of his patron, the habit of seducing light and giddy young ladies, of his own race, into the garden of Queen's Square Place: but tired at last, like Solomon, of pleasures and vanities, he became sedate and thoughtful – took to the church, laid down his knightly title, and was installed as the Reverend John Langborn. He gradually obtained a great reputation for sanctity and learning, and a Doctor's degree was conferred upon him. When I knew him, in his declining days, he bore no other name than the Reverend Doctor John Lanborn; and he was alike conspicuous for his gravity and philosophy. Great respect was invariably shown his reverence: and it was supposed he was not far off from a mitre, when old age interfered with his hopes and honours. He departed amidst the regrets of his many friends, and was gathered to his fathers, and to eternal rest, in a cemetery in Milton's garden.

—*The Works of Jeremy Bentham,* John Bowring

Reneé Stockdale / Animals Animals

CAT OVERBOARD

Thursday, July 11 [1754]

This gale continued till towards noon; when the east end of the island bore but little ahead of us. The captain swaggered and declared he would keep the sea; but the wind got the better of him, so that about three he gave up the victory, and making a sudden tack stood in for the shore, passed by Spithead and Portsmouth, and came to an anchor at a place called Ryde on the island.

A most tragical incident fell out this day at sea. While the ship was under sail, but making as will appear no great way, a kitten, one of four of the feline inhabitants of the cabin, fell from the window into the water: an alarm was immediately given to the captain, who was then upon deck, and received it with the utmost concern and many bitter oaths. He immediately gave orders to the steersman in favour of the poor thing, as he called it; the sails were instantly slackened, and all hands, as the phrase is, employed to recover the poor animal. I was, I own, extremely surprised at all this; less indeed at the captain's extreme tenderness than at his conceiving any possibility of success; for if puss had had nine thousand instead of nine lives, I concluded they had been all lost. The boatswain, however, had more sanguine hopes, for, having stripped himself of his jacket, breeches, and shirt, he leaped boldly into the water, and to my great astonishment in a few minutes returned to the ship, bearing the motionless animal in his mouth. Nor was this, I observed, a matter of such great difficulty as it appeared to my ignorance, and possibly may seem to that of my fresh-water reader. The kitten was now exposed to air and sun on the deck, where its life, of which it retained no symptoms, was despaired of by all.

The captain's humanity, if I may so call it, did not so totally destroy his philosophy as to make him yield himself up to affliction on this melancholy occasion. Having felt his loss like a man, he resolved to shew he could bear it like one; and, having declared he had rather have lost a cask of rum or brandy, betook himself to threshing at backgammon with the Portuguese friar, in which innocent amusement they had passed about two-thirds of their time.

But as I have, perhaps, a little too wantonly endeavoured to raise the tender passions of my readers in this narrative, I should think myself unpardonable if I concluded it without giving them the satisfaction of hearing that the kitten at last recovered, to the great joy of the good captain, but to the great disappointment of some of the sailors, who asserted that the drowning of a cat was the very surest way of raising a favourable wind; a supposition of which, though we have heard several plausible accounts, we will not presume to assign the true original reason.

—*The Journal of a Voyage to Lisbon,* Henry Fielding

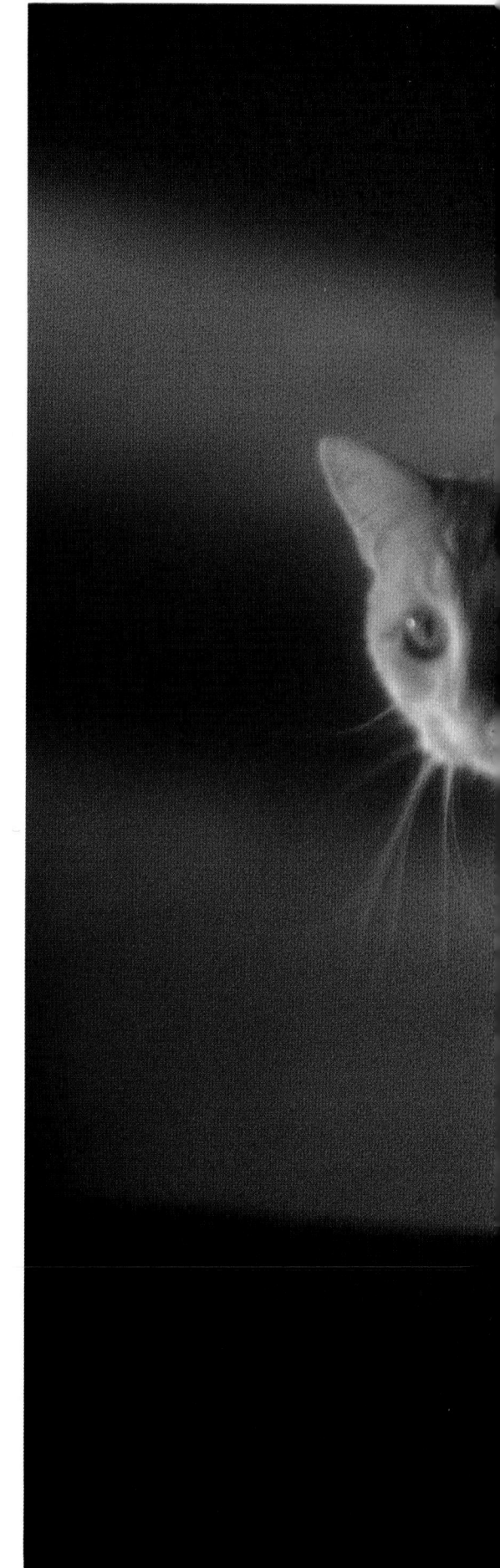

Nicholas Devore III / Photographers Aspen

GRIMALKIN AND THE LEVERET

My friend had a little helpless leveret brought to him, which the servants fed with milk in a spoon, and about the same time his cat kittened and the young were despatched and buried. The hare was soon lost, and supposed to be gone the way of most fondlings, to be killed by some dog or cat. However, in about a fortnight, as the master was sitting in his garden in the dusk of the evening, he observed his cat, with tail erect, trotting towards him, and calling with little short inward notes of complacency, such as they use towards their kittens, and something gamboling after, which proved to be the leveret that the cat had supported with her milk, and continued to support with great affection.

This was a graminivorous animal nurtured by a carniverous and predaceous one!

Why so cruel and sanguinary a beast as a cat, of the ferocious genus of *Felis,* the *murium leo,* as Linnæus calls it, should be affected with any tenderness towards an animal which is its natural prey, is not so easy to determine.

This strange affection probably was occasioned by that desiderium, those tender maternal feelings, which the loss of her kittens had awakened in her breast; and by the complacency and ease she derived to herself from the procuring her teats to be drawn, which were too much distended with milk, till, from habit, she became as much delighted with this fondling as if it had been her real offspring.

This incident is no bad solution of that strange circumstance which grave historians as well as the poets assert, of exposed children being sometimes nurtured by female wild beasts that probably had lost their young. For it is not one whit more marvellous that Romulus and Remus, in their infant state, should be nursed by a she-wolf, than that a poor little sucking leveret should be fostered and cherished by a bloody grimalkin.

—*Natural History of Selborne,* Gilbert White

Nicholas Devore III / Photographers Aspen

THE FIRST SHIP'S CAT

Two sorts of animal, however, left the ark without having entered it. They were the pig and the cat. God had created these animals in the ark for a special purpose. The vessel was becoming full of filth and human excrements and the stench was such that it could no longer be endured. When the inmates went and complained to Noah, he passed his hand down the back of the elephant and the pig issued forth and ate up all the filth that was in the ark. Thereupon the inhabitants of the ark once more came to Noah and complained against the rats who were busy in the ark and caused great nuisance. They ate up all the food and plagued the travellers in many other ways. Noah thereupon passed his hand down the back of the lion. The King of the beasts sneezed and a cat leapt out of its nose. The cat at once ate all the rats and the travellers had peace.

—*Myth and Legend of Ancient Israel*

Nicholas Devore III / Photographers Aspen

CATS

No-one but indefatigable lovers and old
Chilly philosophers can understand the true
Charm of these animals serene and potent, who
Likewise are sedentary and suffer from the cold.

They are the friends of learning and of sexual bliss;
Silence they love, and darkness where temptation breeds.
Erebus would have made them his funereal steeds,
Save that their proud free nature would not stoop to this.

Like those great sphinxes lounging through eternity
In noble attitudes upon the desert sand,
They gaze incuriously at nothing, calm and wise.

Their fecund loins give forth electric flashes, and
Thousands of golden particles drift ceaselessly,
Like galaxies of stars, in their mysterious eyes.
            —*Flowers of Evil,* Charles Baudelaire

MY CAT

When my cat and I entertain each other with mutual antics, as playing with a garter, who knows but that I make more sport for her than she makes for me? Shall I conclude her to be simple that has her time to begin or to refuse to play, as freely as I have mine. Nay, who knows but that it is a defect of my not understanding her language (for doubtless cats can talk and reason with one another) that we agree no better; and who knows but that she pities me for being no wiser than to play with her; and laughs, and censures my folly in making sport for her, when we two play together.

—Montaigne

Margot Conte / Animals Animals

Then how silently and with what a light tread do cats creep up to birds! How stealthily they watch their chance to leap out on tiny mice! They scrape up the earth to bury their droppings, realizing that the smell of these gives them away.

—*Natural History X:94,* Pliny

HIS SERENE HIGHNESS

My dear Daughter,–

Sorry am I to inform you of the illness of his Serene Highness the Archduke Rumpelstilzchen, Marquis Macbum, Earl Tomlemagne, Baron Raticide, Waouhler, and Scratsch. His Serene Highness is afflicted with the mange. One of the ladies of the Kitchen first perceived that he was not in health; and as none of the king's physicians were within reach, they consulted John Edmondson, who, upon hearing the case, pronounced an unfavourable opinion, saying it was a disorder from which few recovered. Acting, however, upon the maxim which, as you may remember, Grio [Grierson, a druggist in Keswick] exhibited in golden letters opposite to his rival's door – *Dum vita spes,* the son of Edmonds prescribed for his Serene Highness that he was to be rubbed with a certain mixture, and take daily a certain quantity of brimstone; and it was thought, after much consideration, that this brimstone could best be taken in boluses, four at a time, each containing about as much as twelve pills.

The physicians would think his Serene Highness an ugly patient, for he has no faith in physic, and he gives no fees, to say nothing of the risk which there is in feeling his pulse. The ladies of the Kitchen, however, are so interested in his welfare, that they have taken upon themselves the arduous task of administering the medicine; which is a matter of great difficulty and some danger, for his Serene Highness rebels against it strongly. Madam Betty takes him on her lap, and holds his head; Madam Mary holds his legs; and Madam Hannah stands ready with a bolus, which is inserted when he opens his mouth for a mournful mew. That painter who was called the Raffaelle of cats would have found the scene a most worthy subject for his pencil. I, who am historiographer to his Serene Highness, feel but too sensibly that I cannot do justice to it in words. But I rejoice to add that the treatment appears to be attended with success, and that visible improvement is observed in the patient.

—*Selections from the Letters of Robert Southey*

Robert Pearcy / Animals Animals

Nicholas Devore III / Photographers Aspen

THE POET'S LAMENTATION FOR THE LOSS OF HIS CAT, WHICH HE USED TO CALL HIS MUSE

Oppress'd with grief in heavy strains I mourn
The partner of my studies from me torn.
How shall I sing? what numbers shall I chuse?
For in my fav'rite cat I've lost my muse.
No more I feel my mind with raptures fired,
I want those airs that Puss so oft inspired;
No crowding thoughts my ready fancy fill,
Nor words run fluent from my easy quill;
Yet shall my verse deplore her cruel fate,
And celebrate the virtues of my cat.

In acts obscene she never took delight;
Nor caterwauls disturbed our sleep by night;
Chaste as a virgin, free from every stain,
And neighb'ring cats mewed for her love in vain.

She never thirsted for the chickens' blood;
Her teeth she only used to chew her food;
Harmless, as satires which her master writes,
A foe to scratching, and unused to bites,
She in the study was my constant mate;
There we together many evenings sat.
Whene'er I felt my towering fancy fail,
I stroked her head, her ears, her back, and tail;
And as I stroked, improved my dying song
From the sweet notes of her melodious tongue:

Her purrs and mews so evenly kept time,
She purred in metre and she mewed in rhyme.
But when my dulness has too stubborn proved,
Nor could by Puss' music be removed,
Oft to the well-known volumes have I gone,
And stole a line from Pope or Addison.
Ofttimes when lost amidst poetic heat,
She leaping on my knee has took her seat;
There saw the throes that rocked my labouring brain,
And licked and clawed me to myself again.

Then, friends, indulge my grief, and let me mourn,
My cat is gone, ah! never to return.
Now in my study, all the tedious night,
Alone I sit, and unassisted write;
Look often round (O greatest cause of pain),
And view the numerous labours of my brain;
Those quires of words arrayed in pompous rhyme,
Which braved the jaws of all-devouring time,
Now undefended and unwatched by cats,
Are doomed a victim to the teeth of rats.

—Joseph Green

A CARGO OF CAT

On the 16th day of June, 1874, the ship *Mary Jane* sailed from Malta, heavily laden with cat. This cargo gave us a good deal of trouble. It was not in bales, but had been dumped into the hold loose. Captain Doble, who had once commanded a ship that carried coals, said he had found that plan the best. When the hold was full of cat the hatch was battened down and we felt good. Unfortunately the mate, thinking the cats would be thirsty, introduced a hose into one of the hatches and pumped in a considerable quantity of water, and the cats of the lower levels were all drowned.

You have seen a dead cat in a pond: you remember its circumference at the waist. Water multiplies the magnitude of a dead cat by ten. On the first day out, it was observed that the ship was much strained. She was three feet wider than usual and as much as ten feet shorter. The convexity of her deck was visibly augmented fore and aft, but she turned up at both ends. Her rudder was clean out of water and she would answer the helm only when running directly against a strong breeze: the rudder, when perverted to one side, would rub against the wind and slew her around; and then she wouldn't steer any more. Owing to the curvature of the keel, the masts came together at the top, and a sailor who had gone up the foremast got bewildered, came down the mizzenmast, looked out over the stern at the receding shores of Malta and shouted: "Land ho!" The ship's fastenings were all giving way; the water on each side was lashed into foam by the tempest of flying bolts that she shed at every pulsation of the cargo. She was quietly wrecking herself without assistance from wind or wave, by the sheer internal energy of feline expansion.

I went to the skipper about it. He was in his favorite position, sitting on the deck, supporting his back against the binnacle, making a V of his legs, and smoking.

"Captain Doble," I said, respectfully touching my hat, which was really not worthy of respect, "this floating palace is afflicted with curvature of the spine and is likewise greatly swollen."

Without raising his eyes he courteously acknowledged my presence by knocking the ashes from his pipe.

"Permit me, Captain," I said, with simple dignity, "to repeat that this ship is much swollen."

"If that is true," said the gallant mariner, reaching for his tobacco pouch, "I think it would be as well to swab her down with liniment. There's a bottle of it in my cabin. Better suggest it to the mate."

"But, Captain, there is no time for empirical treatment; some of the planks at the water line have started."

The skipper rose and looked out over the stern, toward the land; he fixed his eyes on the foaming wake; he gazed into the water to starboard and to port. Then he said:

"My friend, the whole darned thing has started."

Sadly and silently I turned from that obdurate man and walked forward. Suddenly "there was a burst of thunder sound!" The hatch that had held down the cargo was flung whirling into space and sailed in the air like a blown leaf. Pushing upward through the hatchway was a smooth, square column of cat. Grandly and impressively it grew—slowly, serenely, majestically it rose toward the welkin, the relaxing keel parting the mastheads to give it a fair chance. I have stood at Naples and seen Vesuvius painting the town red—from Catania have marked afar, upon the flanks of Ætna, the lava's awful pursuit of the astonished rooster and the despairing pig. The fiery flow from Kilauea's crater, thrusting itself into the forests and licking the entire country clean, is as familiar to me as my mother-tongue. I have seen glaciers, a thousand years old and quite bald, heading for a valley full of tourists at the rate of an inch a month. I have seen a saturated solution of mining camp going down a mountain river, to make a sociable call on the valley farmers. I have stood behind a tree on the battle-field and seen a compact square mile of armed men moving with irresistible momentum to the rear. Whenever anything grand in magnitude or motion is billed to appear I commonly manage to beat my way into the show, and in reporting it I am a man of unscrupulous veracity; but I have seldom observed anything like that solid gray column of Maltese cat!

—Ambrose Bierce

Robert Pearcy / Animals Animals

THE PURGE

'Yes,' said that lady, 'such lace cannot be got now for either love or money; made by the nuns abroad they tell me. They say that they can't make it now, even there. But perhaps they can now they've passed the Catholic Emancipation Bill. I should not wonder. But, in the meantime, I treasure up my lace very much. I daren't even trust the washing of it to my maid' (the little charity school-girl I have named before, but who sounded well as 'my maid'). 'I always wash it myself. And once it had a narrow escape. Of course, your ladyship knows that such lace must never be starched or ironed. Some people wash it in sugar and water; and some in coffee, to make it the right yellow colour; but I myself have a very good receipt for washing it in milk, which stiffens it enough, and gives it a very good creamy colour. Well, ma'am, I had tacked it together (and the beauty of this fine lace is, that when it is wet, it goes into a very little space), and put it to soak in milk, when, unfortunately, I left the room; on my return I found pussy on the table, looking very like a thief, but gulping very uncomfortably as if she was half-choked with something she wanted to swallow, and could not. And, would you believe it? At first I pitied her, and said, "Poor pussy! poor pussy!" till, all at once, I looked and saw the cup of milk empty – cleaned out! "You naughty cat!" said I; and I believe I was provoked enough to give her a slap, which did no good, but only helped the lace down – just as one slaps a choking child on the back. I could have cried, I was so vexed; but I determined I would not give the lace up without a struggle for it. I hoped the lace might disagree with her at any rate; but it would have been too much for Job, if he had seen, as I did, that cat come in, quite placid and purring, not a quarter of an hour after, and almost expecting to be stroked. "No, pussy!" said I; "if you have any conscience, you ought not to expect that!" And then a thought struck me; and I rang the bell for my maid, and sent her to Mr. Hoggins with my compliments, and would he be kind enough to lend me one of his top-boots for an hour? I did not think there was anything odd in the message; but Jenny said, the young men in the surgery laughed as if they would be ill, at my wanting a top-boot. When it came, Jenny and I put pussy in, with her fore-feet straight down, so that they were fastened, and could not scratch, and we gave her a teaspoonful of currant-jelly, in which (your ladyship must excuse me) I had mixed some tartar emetic. I shall never forget how anxious I was for the next half-hour. I took pussy to my own room, and spread a clean towel on the floor. I could have kissed her when she returned the lace to sight, very much as it had gone down. Jenny had boiling water ready, and we soaked it and soaked it, and spread it on a lavender bush in the sun, before I could touch it again, even to put it in milk. But now, your ladyship would never guess that it had been in pussy's inside.'

—*Cranford,* Elizabeth Gaskell

THE WITCH

'Dear friends next door, forgive me this intrusion!
I warn you that a witch can cause confusion
By magically altering her form
Into a beast, to do us men much harm.

Your cat's my wife! Indeed, I am awake!
I'm absolutely sure! I can't mistake
Her scent, her sidelong look, her claws,
Her noisy purr, the way she licks her paws.'

The neighbour and his wife cried out in fear –
'Take back the hussy, we don't want her here!'
Their watch-dog barked and made a frightful row,
But puss, quite unperturbed, said gently, 'Miaow!'

—*Die Hexe,* Heinrich Heine

THE CAT'S DUTY

The animals, by want oppressed,
To man their services addressed:
While each pursued their selfish good,
They hungered for precarious food:
Their hours with anxious cares were vexed;
One day they fed and starved the next:
They saw that plenty, sure and rife,
Was found alone in social life;
That mutual industry professed,
The various wants of man redressed.
The cat, half-famished, lean and weak,
Demands the privilege to speak.
'Well, Puss', says Man, 'and what can you
To benefit the public do?'

The cat replies, 'These teeth, these claws,
With vigilance shall serve the cause,
The mouse destroyed by my pursuit,
No longer shall my feasts pollute;
Nor rats, from nightly ambuscade,
With wasteful teeth your stores invade'.
'I grant', says man, 'to general use
Your parts and talents may conduce;
For rats and mice purloin our grain,
And threshers whirl the flail in vain:
Thus shall the cat, a foe to spoil,
Protect the farmer's honest toil'.

—John Gay

THE RETIRED CAT

A poet's cat, sedate and grave
As poet well could wish to have,
Was much addicted to inquire
For nooks to which she might retire,
And where, secure as mouse in chink,
She might repose, or sit and think.
I know not where she caught the trick,
    Nature perhaps herself had cast her
In such a mould philosophique,
    Or else she learnt it of her master.
Sometimes ascending debonnair,
An apple tree, or lofty pear,
Lodged with convenience in the fork,
She watched the gardener at his work;
Sometimes her ease and solace sought
In an old empty watering-pot,
There, wanting nothing, save a fan,
To seem some nymph in her sedan
Apparelled in exactest sort,
And ready to be borne to court.
    But love of change it seems has place
Not only in our wiser race:
Cats also feel, as well as we,
That passion's force, and so did she.
Her climbing, she began to find,
Exposed her too much to the wind,
And the old utensil of tin
Was cold and comfortless within;
She therefore wished instead of those
Some place of more serene repose,
Where neither cold might come, nor air
Too rudely wanton with her hair,
And sought it in the likeliest mode
Within her master's snug abode.
    A drawer, it chanced, at bottom lined
With linen of the softest kind,
With such as merchants introduce
From India, for the ladies' use,
A drawer impending o'er the rest,
Half open in the topmost chest,
Of depth enough and none to spare,
Invited her to slumber there;
Puss with delight beyond expression
Surveyed the scene and took possession.
Recumbent at her ease ere long,
And lulled by her own humdrum song,
She left the cares of life behind,
And slept as she would sleep her last,
When in came, housewifely inclined,
The chambermaid, and shut it fast.
By no malignity impelled,
But all unconscious whom it held.
    Awakened by the shock, cried Puss,
"Was ever cat attended thus!
The open drawer was left, I see,
Merely to prove a nest for me,
For soon as I was well composed,
Then came the maid and it was closed.
How smooth these kerchiefs and how sweet!
Oh what a delicate retreat!

I will resign myself to rest
Till Sol declining in the west,
Shall call to supper, when, no doubt,
Susan will come and let me out".
    The evening came, the sun descended,
And Puss remained still unattended.
The night rolled tardily away,
(With her indeed 'twas never day);
The sprightly morn her course renewed,
The evening gray again ensued,
And Puss came into mind no more
Than if entombed the day before.
With hunger pinched, and pinched for room,
She now presaged approaching doom,
Nor slept a single wink, or purred,
Conscious of jeopardy incurred.
    That night, by chance, the poet watching,
Heard an inexplicable scratching;
His noble heart went pit-a-pat,
And to himself he said, "What's that?"
He drew the curtain at his side,
And forth he peeped, but nothing spied.
Yet, by his ear directed, guessed
Something imprisoned in the chest,
And, doubtful what, with prudent care
Resolved it should continue there.
At length, a voice which well he knew,
A long and melancholy mew,
Saluting his poetic ears,
Consoled him, and dispelled his fears:
He left his bed, he trod the floor,
He 'gan in haste the drawers explore,
The lowest first, and without stop
The rest in order to the top.
For 'tis a truth well known to most,
That whatsoever thing is lost,
We seek it, ere it come to light,
In every cranny but the right.
Forth skipped the cat, not how replete
As erst with airy self-conceit,
Nor in her own fond apprehension
A theme for all the world's attention,
But modest, sober, cured of all
Her notions hyperbolical,
And wishing for a place of rest
Anything rather than a chest.
Then stepped the poet into bed
With this reflection in his head:

MORAL

Beware of too sublime a sense
Of your own worth and consequence.
The man who dreams himself so great,
And his importance of such weight,
That all around in all that's done,
Must move and act for him alone,
Will learn in school of tribulation
The folly of his expectation.

—William Cowper

Nicholas Devore III / Photographers Aspen

THE VAIN CAT

Remarked a Tortoise to a Cat:
"Your speed's a thing to marvel at!
I saw you as you flitted by,
And wished I were one-half so spry."
The Cat said, humbly: "Why, indeed
I was not showing then my speed—
That was a poor performance." Then
She said exultantly (as when
The condor feels his bosom thrill
Remembering Chimborazo's hill,
and how he soared so high above,
It looked a valley, he a dove):
" 'Twould fire your very carapace
To see me with a dog in chase!"
Its snout in any kind of swill,
Pride, like a pig, will suck its fill.
                              —Ambrose Bierce

NOBLE PLEASURES

It is the misfortune of cats, that they are generally brought into contrast with dogs, whose fidelity, attachment, and sagacity are so often subjects of admiration. But it is obviously unfair to bring into comparison animals differently constituted, and dissimilar both in their pretensions and capabilities. Mankind, in such estimates, are apt, besides, to be influenced by selfish motives, and to applaud those qualities only which minister to their own interest, importance, or gratification. The character of the dog, for example, however admirable in our own eyes, would, *if viewed in a universal spirit,* be open to impeachment. His attachment and fidelity are certainly very gratifying, so far as *we* are concerned; but it cannot be denied, that he is a *traitor to his own order,* and a terror, not to speak of a disgrace, to all his four-footed connexions. He abandons his kind, and becomes the willing slave and fawning parasite of man — ready to wage war with every creature, his own tribe not excepted. There is no indignity, whether of lash or kick, from the hands of his master, to which he will object, and no paltry office, not even that of turnspit, too humiliating for him to fulfil. He will go crouching through the fields to point out poor partridges for destruction, and condescend to watch wood-yards with a chain about his neck, as if he had a standing interest in fir deals and splinters! Look if the cat will so far forget her natural dignity, or outrage any of her inherent propensities, for the gratification of man. *She* is connected with royalty, the head of her family being the lion, the king of the forest — and she therefore appropriately leads a luxurious life, having a proper aristocratic indifference to every thing which does not minister to her own pleasure. It must be from her relationship that the adage has arisen, 'A cat may look at a king.'

Like the rest of the nobility, she is much given to hunting, birding, and fishing, but hates all other sorts of exertion. When not engaged in the chase after 'mice and such small deer,' she loiters by the fireside, on chair or sofa, humming a tune, in falsetto voice, or feeling with her paw the length of her whiskers.

—*Interesting Anecdotes of the Animal Kingdom,* Thomas Brown

A CAT AND BULL STORY

'Wickham,' retorted Mrs. Pipchin, colouring, 'is a wicked, impudent bold-faced hussy.'

'What's that?' inquired Paul.

'Never you mind, Sir,' retorted Mrs. Pipchin. 'Remember the story of the little boy that was gored to death by a mad bull, for asking questions.'

'If the bull was mad,' said Paul, 'how did *he* know the boy had asked questions? Nobody can go and whisper secrets to a mad bull. I don't believe that story.'

'You don't believe it, Sir?' repeated Mrs. Pipchin amazed.

'No,' said Paul.

'Not if it should happen to have been a tame bull, you little Infidel?' said Mrs. Pipchin.

As Paul had not considered the subject in that light, and had founded his conclusions on the alleged lunacy of the bull, he allowed himself to be put down for the present. But he sat turning it over in his mind, with such an obvious intention of fixing Mrs. Pipchin presently, that even that hardy old lady deemed it prudent to retreat until he should have forgotten the subject.

From that time, Mrs. Pipchin appeared to have something of the same odd kind of attraction towards Paul, as Paul had towards her. She would make him move his chair to her side of the fire, instead of sitting opposite; and there he would remain in a nook between Mrs. Pipchin and the fender, with all the light of his little face absorbed into the black bombazeen drapery, studying every line and wrinkle of her countenance, and peering at the hard grey eye, until Mrs. Pipchin was sometimes fain to shut it on pretence of dozing. Mrs. Pipchin had an old black cat, who generally lay coiled upon the centre foot of the fender, purring egotistically, and winking at the fire until the contracted pupils of his eyes were like two notes of admiration. The good old lady might have been – not to record it disrespectfully – a witch, and Paul and the cat her two familiars, as they all sat by the fire together. It would have been quite in keeping with the appearance of the party if they had all sprung up the chimney in a high wind one night, and never been heard of any more.

This, however, never came to pass. The cat, and Paul, and Mrs. Pipchin, were constantly to be found in their usual places after dark; and Paul, eschewing the companionship of Master Bitherstone, went on studying Mrs. Pipchin, and the cat, and the fire, night after night, as if they were a book of necromancy, in three volumes.

—*Dombey and Son,* Charles Dickens

'THE CAT WITH WINGS'

You never saw a cat with wings,
I'll bet a dollar – well, I did;
'Twas one of those fantastic things
One runs across in old Madrid.
A walloping big tom it was,
(Maybe of the Angora line,)
With silken ears and velvet paws,
And silver hair, superbly fine.

It sprawled upon a crimson mat,
Yet though crowds came to gaze on it,
It was a supercilious cat,
And didn't seem to mind a bit.
It looked at us with dim disdain,
And indolently seemed to sigh:
'There's not another cat in Spain
One half so marvellous as I.'

Its owner gently stroked its head,
And tickled it with fingers light.
'Ah no, it cannot fly,' he said;
'But see – it has the *wings* all right.'
Then tenderly from off its back
He raised, despite its feline fears,
Appendages that seemed to lack
Vitality – like rabbit's ears.

And then the vision that I had
Of Tabbie soaring through the night,
Quick vanished, and I felt so sad
For that poor pussy's piteous plight.
For though frustration has its stings,
Its mockeries in Hope's despite,
The hell of hells is to have wings
Yet be denied the bliss of flight.
                    —Robert W. Service

Robert Pearcy / Animals Animals

Patti Murray / Animals Animals

THE WIDOW AND HER CAT
A FABLE

A widow kept a favourite cat,
At first a gentle creature;
But, when he was grown sleek and fat,
With many a mouse, and many a rat,
He soon disclosed his nature.

The fox and he were friends of old,
Nor could they now be parted;
They nightly slunk to rob the fold,
Devoured the lambs, the fleeces sold;
And Puss grew lion-hearted.

He scratched her maid, he stole the cream,
He tore her best laced pinner;
Nor Chanticleer upon the beam,
Nor chick, nor duckling 'scapes, when Grim
Invites the fox to dinner.

The dame full wisely did decree,
For fear he should dispatch more,
That the false wretch should worried be;
But in a saucy manner he
Thus speeched it like a Lechmere:

"Must I, against all right and law,
Like pole-cat vile be treated?
I, who so long with tooth and claw,
Have kept domestic mice in awe,
And foreign foes defeated.

Your golden pippins, and your pies,
How oft have I defended!
'Tis true, the pinner which you prize,
I tore in frolic; to your eyes
I never harm intended.

63

LISY'S PARTING WITH HER CAT

The dreadful hour with solemn pace approach'd,
Lash'd fiercely on by unrelenting fate,
When Lisy and her bosom Cat must part;
For now, to school and pensive needle doom'd,
She's banish'd from her childhood's undash'd joy,
And all the pleasing intercourse she kept
With her gray comrade, which has often soothed
Her tender moments, while the world around
Glow'd with ambition, business, and vice,
Or lay dissolved in sleep's delicious arms;
And from their dewy orbs the conscious stars
Shed on their friendship influence benign.

But see where mournful Puss, advancing, stood
With outstretch'd tail, cast looks of anxious woe
On melting Lisy, in whose eye the tears
Stood tremulous, and thus would fain have said,
If nature had not tied her struggling tongue: —
"Unkind, oh! who shall now with fattening milk,
With flesh, with bread, with fish beloved, and meat,
Regale my taste? and at the cheerful fire,
Ah! who shall bask me in their downy lap?
Who shall invite me to the bed, and throw
The bedclothes o'er me in the winter night,
When Eurus roars? Beneath whose soothing hand
Soft shall I purr? But now, when Lisy's gone,
What is the dull, officious world to me?
I loathe the thoughts of life": thus plain'd the Cat,
While Lisy felt, by sympathetic touch,
The anxious thoughts that in her mind revolved,
And casting on her a desponding look,
She snatch'd her in her arms with eager grief
And mewing, thus began:—"O Cat beloved!
Thou dear companion of my tender years!
Joy of my youth! that oft hast lick'd my hands
With velvet tongue ne'er stain'd by mouse's blood;
Oh, gentle Cat! how shall I part with thee?

How dead and heavy will the moments pass
When you are not in my delighted eye,
With Cubi playing, or your flying tail!
How harshly will the softest muslin feel,
And all the silk of schools, while I no more
Have your sleek skin to soothe my soften'd sense!
How shall I eat while you are not beside
To share the bit? How shall I ever sleep
While I no more your lulling murmurs hear?
Yet we must part—so rigid fate decrees—
But never shall your loved idea, dear,
Part from my soul, and when I first can mark
The embroider'd figure on the snowy lawn,
Your image shall my needle keen employ.
Hark! now I'm call'd away! O direful sound!
I come—I come, but first I charge you all—
You, you, and you,—particularly you,
O Mary, Mary, feed her with the best,
Repose her nightly in the warmest couch,
And be a Lisy to her!"—Having said,
She sat her down, and with her head across,
Rush'd to the evil which she could not shun,
While a sad mew went knelling to her heart!

—James Thomson

Nicholas Devore III / Photographers Aspen

Nicholas Devore III / Photographers Aspen

THE CUNNINGEST KITTEN

White House, Jan. 6, 1903

Dear Kermit,

We felt very melancholy after you and Ted left and the house seemed empty and lonely. But it was the greatest possible comfort to feel that you both really have enjoyed school and are both doing well there.

Tom Quartz is certainly the cunningest kitten I have ever seen. He is always playing pranks on Jack and I get very nervous lest Jack should grow too irritated. The other evening they were both in the library – Jack sleeping before the fire – Tom Quartz scampering about, an exceedingly playful little wild creature – which is about what he is. He would race across the floor, then jump upon the curtain or play with the tassel. Suddenly he spied Jack and galloped up to him. Jack, looking exceedingly sullen and shame-faced, jumped out of the way and got upon the sofa, where Tom Quartz instantly jumped upon him again. Jack suddenly shifted to the other sofa, where Tom Quartz again went after him. Then Jack started for the door, while Tom made a rapid turn under the sofa and around the table, and just as Jack reached the door leaped on his hind-quarters. Jack bounded forward and away and the two went tandem out of the room – Jack not reappearing at all; and after about five minutes Tom Quartz stalked solemnly back.

Another evening the next Speaker of the House, Mr. Cannon, an exceedingly solemn, elderly gentleman with chin whiskers, who certainly does not look to be of playful nature, came to call upon me. He is a great friend of mine, and we sat talking over what our policies for the session should be until about eleven o'clock; and when he went away I accompanied him to the head of the stairs. He had gone about half-way down when Tom Quartz strolled by, his tail erect and very fluffy. He spied Mr. Cannon going down the stairs, jumped to the conclusion that he was a playmate escaping, and raced after him, suddenly grasping him by the leg the way he does Archie and Quentin when they play hide and seek with him; then loosening his hold he tore downstairs ahead of Mr. Cannon, who eyed him with iron calm and not one particle of surprise . . .

—*Theodore Roosevelt's Letters to His Children*

THE CAT THAT WALKED BY HIMSELF

'O my Enemy and Wife of my Enemy and Mother of my Enemy,' said the Cat, 'is that little mouse part of your Magic?'

'Ouh! Chee! No indeed!' said the Woman, and she dropped the blade-bone and jumped upon the footstool in front of the fire and braided up her hair very quick for fear that the mouse should run up it.

'Ah,' said the Cat, watching. 'then the mouse will do me no harm if I eat it?'

'No,' said the Woman, braiding up her hair, 'eat it quickly and I will ever be grateful to you.'

Cat made one jump and caught the little mouse, and the Woman said, 'A hundred thanks. Even the First Friend is not quick enough to catch little mice as you have done. You must be very wise.'

That very minute and second, O Best Beloved, the Milk-pot that stood by the fire cracked in two pieces – *ffft!* – because it remembered the bargain she had made with the Cat; and when the Woman jumped down from the footstool – lo and behold! – the Cat was lapping up the warm white milk that lay in one of the broken pieces.

'O my Enemy and Wife of my Enemy and Mother of my Enemy,' said the Cat, 'it is I: for you have spoken three words in my praise, and now I can drink the warm white milk three times a day for always and always and always. But *still* I am the Cat who walks by himself, and all places are alike to me.'

Then the Woman laughed and set the Cat a bowl of the warm white milk and said, 'O Cat, you are as clever as a man.'

—*Just So Stories,* Rudyard Kipling

CATS

All ardent lovers and all sages prize,
– As ripening years incline upon their brows –
The mighty and mild cats – pride of the house –
That like unto them are indolent, stern and wise.

The friends of Learning and of Ecstasy,
They search for silence and the horrors of gloom;
The Devil had used them for his steeds of doom,
Could he alone have bent their pride to slavery.

When, musing, they display their outlines chaste,
Of the great sphinxes – stretched o'er the sandy waste,
That seem to slumber deep in a dream without end:

From out their loins a fountainous furnace flies,
And grains of sparkling gold, as fine as sand,
Bestir the mystic pupils of their eyes.
                                        —Charles Baudelaire

Gerard Lacz / Animals Animals

Henry Ausloos / Animals Animals

It is easy to understand why the rabble dislike cats.
A cat is beautiful; it suggests ideas of luxury, cleanliness, voluptuous pleasures.

—Charles Baudelaire

Frank Balthis

'THE BLACK CAT'

We had birds, gold-fish, a fine dog, rabbits, a small monkey, and *a cat*.

This latter was a remarkably large and beautiful animal, entirely black, and sagacious to an astonishing degree. In speaking of his intelligence, my wife, who at heart was not a little tinctured with superstition, made frequent allusion to the ancient popular notion which regarded all black cats as witches in disguise. Not that she was ever *serious* upon this point, and I mention the matter at all for no better reason than that it happens just now to be remembered.

Pluto – this was the cat's name – was my favourite pet and playmate. I alone fed him, and he attended me wherever I went about the house. It was even with difficulty that I could prevent him from following me through the streets.

Our friendship lasted in this manner for several years, during which my general temperament and character – through the instrumentality of the Fiend Intemperance – had (I blush to confess it) experienced a radical alteration for the worse.

—Edgar Allan Poe

69

Gerard Lacz / Animals Animals

WORSHIPPING GINGER

Though my mother could never teach me to read, she taught me hymns and poetry by rote, which incited me to write rhymes on my own account. I had many favourites among cats, dogs and birds, my mother's reprobation and the servants' nuisance; but I turned them all to account and wove them into stories, to which I tried to give as much personal interest as old Mother Hubbard bestowed on her dog.

The head favourite of my menagerie was a magnificent and very intelligent cat, 'Ginger,' by name, from the colour of her coat, which though almost orange was very much admired. She was the last of a race of cats sacred in the traditions of the Music Hall. Pat Brennan, '*The sad historian of the ruined towers,*' held them in the greatest reverence mingled with superstitious awe. Brennan was a good Catholic, but rather given to exaggeration, which rendered his testimony to matters of fact proverbially questionable; and it became a bye word among unbelieving neighbours when any one told a wonderful story, to ask, 'Do you know Brennan? Well, then, enough said!' After this, there was nothing left for the disconcerted narrator but to walk away. One of his stories was – that the monastic cats had *stings* in their tails, which after their death were preserved by the monks for purposes of flagellation, or by the nuns – Brennan was not sure which!

Ginger was as much the object of my idolatry as if she had had a temple and I had been a worshipper in ancient Egypt; but, like other deities, she was reprobated by those who were not of my faith.

I made her up a nice little cell, under the beaufet, as side-boards were then called in Ireland – a sort of alcove cut out of the wall of our parlour where the best glass and the family 'bit of plate' – a silver tankard – with the crest of the Hills upon it (a dove with an olive branch in its mouth), which commanded great respect in our family.

Ginger's sly attempt to hide herself from my mother, to whom she had that antipathy which animals so often betray to particular individuals,

were a source of great amusement to my little sister and myself; but when she chose the retreat of the beaufet as the scene of her *accouchement,* our fear lest it should come to my mother's knowledge, was as great as if we had been concealing a moral turpitude.

It was a good and pious custom of my mother's to hear us our prayers every night; when Molly tapped at the parlour door at nine o'clock, we knelt at my mother's feet, our four little hands clasped in her's, and our eyes turned to her with looks of love, as they repeated that simple and beautiful invocation, the Lord's Prayer; to this was always added the supplication, 'Lighten our darkness we beseech Thee;' after which we were accustomed to recite a prayer of our affectionate suggestion, calling a blessing on the heads of all we knew and loved, which ran thus, 'God bless papa, mamma, my dear sister, and Molly, and Betty, and Joe, and James, and all our good friends.' One night, however, before my mother could pronounce her solemn 'amen,' a soft muttered 'purr' issued from the cupboard, my heart echoed the appeal, and I added, 'God bless Ginger the cat!' Wasn't my mother shocked! She shook both my shoulders and said, 'What do you mean by that, you stupid child?'

'May I not say, "Bless Ginger?" ' I asked humbly.

'Certainly *not,*' said my mother emphatically.

'Why, mamma?'

'Because Ginger is not a Christian.'

'*Why* is not Ginger a Christian?'

'Why? because Ginger is only an animal.'

'Am I a Christian, mamma, or an animal?'

'I will not answer any more foolish questions tonight. Molly, take these children to bed, and do teach Sydney not to ask those silly questions.'

So we were sent off in disgrace, but not before I had given Ginger a wink, whose bright eyes acknowledged the salute through the half-open door.

The result of this was that I tried my hand at a poem.

The jingle of rhyme was familiar to my ear

through my mother's constant recitation of verses, from the sublime Universal Prayer of the Pope to the nursery rhyme of Little Jack Horner; whilst my father's dramatic citations, which had descended even to the servants, had furnished me with the tags of plays from Shakespeare to O'Keefe; so that 'I lisped in numbers' though the numbers never came.

Here is my first attempt:

My dear pussy cat,
Were I a mouse or rat,
  Sure I never would run off from you,
You're so funny and gay,
With your tail when you play,
  And no song is so sweet as your 'mew;'
But pray keep in your press,
And don't make a mess,
  When you share with your kittens our posset;
For mamma can't abide you,
And I cannot hide you,
  Except you keep close in your closet!

I tagged these doggrels together while lying awake half the night, and as soon as I could get a hearing in the morning I recited them to the kitchen, and no elocution ever pronounced in *that* kitchen (although it was dedicated to Melpomene, whose image shone on an orchestra that had been converted into a dresser, the whole apartment being the remains of the fantastic Ridotto, though now being converted to culinary purposes in the same floor as our dining-room), no elocution had ever excited more applause. James undertook to write it down, and Molly corrected the press. It was served up at breakfast to my father, and it not only procured me his rapturous praise but my mother's forgiveness.

My father took me to Moira House; made me recite my poem, to which he had taught me to add appropriate emphasis and action, to which my own tendency to grimace added considerable comicality. The Countess of Moira laughed heartily at the 'infant Muse' as my father called me, and ordered the housekeeper to send up a large plate of bread and jam, the earliest recompense of my literary labours.

—*Lady Morgan's Memoirs,* Sydney, Lady Morgan

George F. Godfrey / Animals Animals

THE CHESHIRE-CAT SPEAKS

The baby grunted again, and Alice looked very anxiously into its face to see what was the matter with it. There could be no doubt that it had a *very* turn-up nose, much more like a snout than a real nose: also its eyes were getting extremely small for a baby: altogether Alice did not like the look of the thing at all. 'But perhaps it was only sobbing,' she thought, and looked into its eyes again, to see if there were any tears.

No, there were no tears. 'If you're going to turn into a pig, my dear,' said Alice, seriously, 'I'll have nothing more to do with you. Mind now!' The poor little thing sobbed again (or grunted, it was impossible to say which), and they went on for some while in silence.

Alice was just beginning to think to herself, 'Now, what am I to do with this creature, when I get it home?' when it grunted again, so violently, that she looked down into its face in some alarm. This time there could be *no* mistake about it: it was neither more or less than a pig, and she felt that it would be quite absurd for her to carry it any further.

So she set the little creature down, and felt quite relieved to see it trot away quietly into the wood. 'If it had grown up,' she said to herself, 'it would have made a dreadfully ugly child: but it makes rather a handsome pig, I think.' And she began thinking over other children she knew, who might do very well as pigs, and was just saying to herself 'if one only knew the right way to change them – ' when she was a little startled by seeing the Cheshire-Cat sitting on a bough of a tree a few yards off.

The Cat only grinned when it saw Alice. It looked good-natured, she thought: still it had *very* long claws and a great many teeth, so she felt that it ought to be treated with respect.

'Cheshire-Puss,' she began rather timidly, as she did not at all know whether it would like the name: however, it only grinned a little wider. 'Come, it's pleased so far,' thought Alice, and she went on. 'Would you tell me, please, which way I ought to go from here?'

'That depends a good deal on where you want to get to,' said the Cat.

'I don't much care where – ' said Alice.

'Then it doesn't matter which way you go,' said the Cat.

' – so long as I get *somewhere*,' said Alice.

'Oh, you're sure to do that,' said the Cat, 'if you only walk long enough.'

Alice felt that this could not be denied, so she tried another question. 'What sort of people live about here?'

'In *that* direction,' the Cat said, waving its right paw round, 'lives a Hatter: and in *that* direction,' waving the other paw, 'lives a March Hare. Visit either you like: they're both mad.'

'But I don't want to go among mad people,' Alice remarked.

Oh, you ca'n't help that,' said the Cat: 'We're all mad here. I'm mad. You're mad.'

'How do you know I'm mad?' said Alice.

'You must be,' said the Cat, 'or you wouldn't have come here.'

Alice didn't think that proved it at all: however, she went on: 'And how do you know that you're mad?'

'To begin with,' said the Cat, 'a dog's not mad. You grant that?'

'I suppose so,' said Alice.

'Well, then,' the Cat went on, 'you see a dog growls when it's angry, and wags its tail when it's pleased. Now *I* growl when I'm pleased, and wag my tail when I'm angry. Therefore I'm mad.'

'*I* call it purring, not growling,' said Alice.

'Call it what you like,' said the Cat. 'Do you play croquet with the Queen to-day?'

'I should like it very much,' said Alice, 'but I haven't been invited yet.'

'You'll see me there,' said the Cat, and vanished.

Alice was not much surprised at this, she was getting so well used to queer things happening. While she was still looking at the place where it had been, it suddenly appeared again.

'By-the-bye, what became of the baby?' said the Cat. 'I'd nearly forgotten to ask.'

'It turned into a pig,' Alice answered very quietly, just as if the Cat had come back in a natural way.

'I thought it would,' said the Cat, and vanished again.

Alice waited a little, half expecting to see it again, but it did not appear, and after a minute or two she walked on in the direction in which the March Hare was said to live. 'I've seen hatters before,' she said to herself: 'the March Hare will be much the most interesting, and perhaps, as this is May, it wo'n't be raving mad – at least not so mad as it was in March.' As she said this, she looked up, and there was the Cat again, sitting on a branch of a tree.

'Did you say "pig", or "fig"?' said the Cat.

'I said "pig",' replied Alice; 'and I wish you wouldn't keep appearing, and vanishing so suddenly: you make one quite giddy!'

'All right,' said the Cat; and this time it vanished quite slowly, beginning with the end of the tail, and ending with the grin, which remained some time after the rest of it had gone.

'Well! I've often seen a cat without a grin,' thought Alice, 'but a grin without a cat! It's the most curious thing I ever saw in all my life!'

—*Alice's Adventures in Wonderland*, Lewis Carroll

HINSE OF HINSFELDT

I have added a most romantic inmate to my family a large blood-hound allowed to be the finest dog of the kind in Scotland perfectly gentle affectionate and good-natured and the darling of all the children. I had him in a present from Glengarry who has refused the breed to people of the very first rank. He is between the deer greyhound and mastiff with a shaggy mane like a lion and always sits beside me at dinner – his head as high as the back of my chair. Yet it will gratify you to know that a favourite cat keeps him in the greatest possible order insists upon all rights of precedence and scratches with impunity the nose of an animal who would make no bones of a wolf and pulls down a red-deer without fear or difficulty. I heard my friend set up some most piteous howls and I assure you the noise was no joke – all occasioned by his fear of passing puss who had stationed himself on the stairs.

The young bloodhound Nimrod has dispatched poor old Hinzie the stoutness of whose heart led him always to attack the mighty huntsman before the Lord till at last he paid the kain as we say.

From a hermit you can expect little news. The worst is that the new bloodhound has killed Walters friend old Hinzie the cat. I must say Hinzie had been the aggressor in former encounters but I was vexed to lose my old friend.

I . . . was rather amused with Mrs. Baillie's cat who worried the dog. It is just like her Mrs. who beats the male race of authors out of the pitt in describing the higher passions that are more proper to their sex than hers. Alack a day my poor cat Hinze my acquaintance and in some sort my friend of fifteen years was snaped at once by the paynim Nimrod. What could I say to him but what Brantome said to some *fouilleur* who had been too successful in a duel 'Ah mon grand ami vous avez tué mon autre grand ami.' It is a good thing to have read queer books they always furnish you with a parallel case in your afflictions.

—Sir Walter Scott

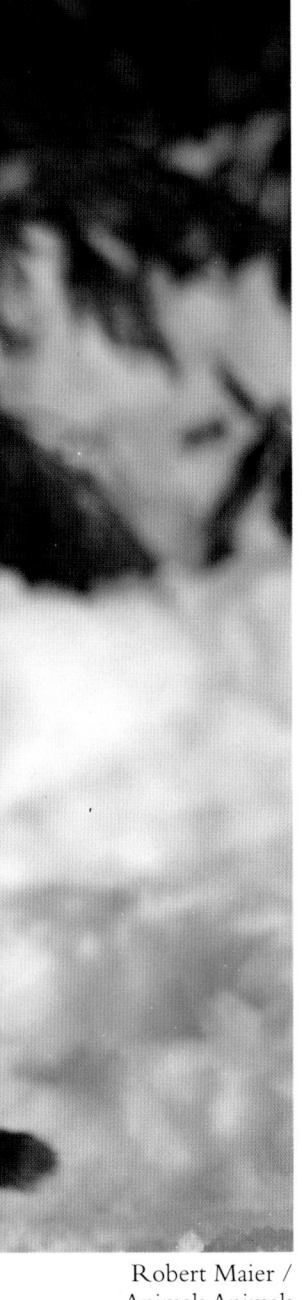

BOWS AND CURTSEYS

My child, we were two children,
Small, merry by childhood's law;
We used to crawl to the hen-house
And hide ourselves in the straw.

We crowed like cocks, and whenever
The passers near us drew –
Cock-a-doodle! they thought
'Twas a real cock that crew.

The boxes about our courtyard
We carpeted to our mind,
And lived there both together –
Kept house in a noble kind.

The neighbour's old cat often
Came to pay us a visit;
We made her a bow and curtsey,
Each with a compliment in it.

After her health we asked,
Our care and regard to evince –
(We have made the very same speeches
To many an old cat since).
              —Elizabeth Barrett Browning

Robert Maier /
Animals Animals

Nicholas Devore III / Photographers Aspen

73

Nicholas Devore III / Photographers Aspen

THE GOODWIFE'S METAMORPHOSIS

The same day, another hero, celebrated for his hatred of witchcraft, was warming himself in his hunting hut, in the forest of Gaick in Badenoch. His faithful hounds, fatigued with the morning chase, lay stretched on the turf by his side, – his gun, that would not miss, reclined in the neuk of the boothy, – the *skian dhu* of the sharp edge hung by his side, and these alone constituted his company. As the hunter sat listening to the howling storm as it whistled by, there entered at the door an apparently poor weather-beaten cat, shivering with cold, and drenched to the skin. On observing her, the hairs of the dogs became erected bristles, and they immediately rose to attack the pitiable cat, which stood trembling at the door. 'Great hunter of the hills,' exclaims the poor-looking trembling cat, 'I claim your protection. I know your hatred to my craft, and perhaps it is just. Still spare, oh spare a poor jaded wretch, who thus flies to you for protection from the cruelty and oppression of her sisterhood.' Moved to compassion by her eloquent address, and disdaining to take advantage of his greatest enemy in such a seemingly forlorn situation, he pacified his infuriated dogs, and desired her to come forward to the fire and warm herself. 'Nay,' says she, 'in the first place, you will please bind with this long hair those two furious hounds of yours, for I am afraid they will tear my poor hams to pieces. I pray you, therefore, my dear sir, that you would have the goodness to bind them together by the necks with this long hair.' But the curious nature of the hair induced the hunter to dissemble a little. Instead of having bound his dogs with it, as he pretended, he threw it across a beam of wood which connected the couple of the boothy. The witch then supposing the dogs securely bound, approached the fire, and squatted herself down as if to dry herself. She had not sitten many minutes, when the hunter could easily discover a striking increase in her size, which he could not forbear remarking in a jocular manner to herself. 'A bad death to you, you nasty beast,' says the hunter; 'you are getting very large.' – 'Aye, aye,' replied the cat, equally jocosely, 'as my hairs imbibe the heat, they naturally expand.' These jokes, however, were but a prelude to a more serious conversation. The cat still continuing her growth, had at length attained a most extraordinary size, – when, in the twinkling of an eye, she transformed herself into her proper likeness of the Goodwife of Laggan, and thus addressed him: 'Hunter of the Hills, your hour of reckoning is arrived. Behold me before you, the avowed champion of my devoted sisterhood, of whom Macgillichallum of Razay and you were always the most relentless enemies. But Razay is no more. His last breath is fled. He lies a lifeless corpse on the bottom of the main; and now, Hunter of the Hills, it is your turn.' With these words, assuming a most hideous and terrific appearance, she made a spring at the hunter. The two

dogs, which she supposed securely bound by the infernal hair, sprung at her in her turn, and a most furious conflict ensued. The witch, thus unexpectedly attacked by the dogs, now began to repent of her temerity. '*Fasten, hair, fasten,*' she perpetually exclaimed, supposing the dogs to have been bound by the hair; and so effectually did the hair *fasten,* according to her order, that it at last snapt the beam in twain. At length, finding herself completely overpowered, she attempted a retreat, but so closely were the hounds fastened in her breasts, that it was with no small difficulty she could get herself disengaged from them. Screaming and shrieking, the Wife of Laggan dragged herself out of the house, trailing after the dogs, which were fastened in her so closely, that they never loosed their hold until she demolished every tooth in their heads. Then metamorphosing herself into the likeness of a raven, she fled over the mountains in the direction of her home. The two faithful dogs, bleeding and exhausted, returned to their master, and, in the act of caressing his hand, both fell down and expired at his feet. Regretting their loss with a sorrow only known to the parent who weeps over the remains of departed children, he buried his devoted dogs, and returned to his family. His wife was not in the house when he arrived, but she soon made her appearance. 'Where hae you been, my love?' inquired the husband. – 'Indeed,' replies she, 'I have been seeing the Goodwife of Laggan, who has been just seized with so severe an illness, that she is not expected to live for any time.' – 'Aye! aye!' says he, 'what is the matter with the worthy woman?' – 'She was all day absent in the moss at her peats,' replies the wife, 'and was seized with a sudden colic, in consequence of getting wet feet, and now all her friends and neighbours are expecting her demision.' – 'Poor woman,' says the husband, 'I am sorry for her. Get me some dinner, it will be right that I should go and see her also.' Dinner being provided and dispatched, the hunter immediately proceeded to the house of Laggan, where he found a great assemblage of neighbours mourning, with great sincerity, the approaching decease of a woman whom they all had hitherto esteemed virtuous. The hunter, walking up to the sick woman's bed in a rage, proportioned to the greatness of its cause, stripped the sick woman of all her coverings. A shriek from the now exposed witch brought all the company around her. 'Behold,' says he, 'the object of your solicitude, who is nothing less than an infernal witch. To-day, she informs me, she was present at the death of the Laird of Razay, and only a few hours have elapsed since she attempted to make me share his fate. This night, however, she shall expiate her crime, by the forfeiture of her horrid life.'

—*The Popular Superstitions and Festive Amusements of the Highlanders of Scotland,* William Grant Stewart

Nicholas Devore III / Photographers Aspen

A CAT

Philosopher and comrade, not for thee
The fond and foolish love which binds the dog;
Only a quiet sympathy which sees
Through all my faults and bears with them awhile.
Be lenient still, and have some faith in me,
Gentlest of skeptics, sleepiest of friends.

—Jules Lemaître

CATS AND PRINCES
VERY MUCH ALIKE

"A cat who from a window peepeth out,
Is very like a Cat who peepeth in"–
Thus is it said – and he who is no lout,
Knoweth that Cats are unto Men akin.

—Peter Pindar

AN APPEAL TO CATS IN THE
BUSINESS OF LOVE

Ye Cats that at midnight spit love at each other,
Who best feel the pangs of a passionate lover,
I appeal to your scratches and your tattered fur,
If the business of love be no more than to purr.

—Thomas Flatman

THE CAT AND THE RAIN

Careful observers may foretell the hour
(By sure prognostics) when to dread a shower;
While rain depends, the pensive cat gives o'er
Her frolics, and pursues her tail no more.

—Jonathan Swift

Robert Maier / Animals Animals

A NOISE AND A WAWLING
An extract from what is sometimes referred to as 'the first English novel.'

I would counsel all men to bury or burn all executed bodies, and refrain from making such abhominable sacrifice as I have often seen, with ravens or rather devils feeding upon them, in this foresaid leads – in the which every night many cats assembled, and there made such a noise that I could not sleep for them.

Wherefore, on a time as I was sitting by the fire with certain of the house, I told them what a noise and what a wawling the cats had made there the night before from ten o'clock till one, so that neither I could sleep nor study for them; and by means of this introduction we fell in communication of cats. And some affirming, as I do now (but I was against it then), that they had understanding, for confirmation whereof one of the servants told this story.

'There was in my country,' quod he, 'a man' (the fellow was born in Staffordshire) 'that had a young cat which he had brought up of a kitling, and would nightly dally and play with it; and on a time as he rode through Kankwood about certain business, a cat, as he thought, leaped out of a bush before him and called him twice or thrice by his name. But because he made none answer nor spake (for he was so afraid that he could not), she spake to him plainly twice or thrice these words following: "Commend me unto Titton Tatton and to Puss thy Catton, and tell her that Grimalkin is dead." This done she went her way, and the man went forward about his business. And after that he was returned home, in an evening sitting by the fire with his wife and his household, he told of his adventure in the wood. And when he had told them all the cat's message, his cat, which had harkened unto the tale, looked upon him sadly, and at the last said, 'And is Grimalkin dead? Then farewell dame," and therewith went her way and was never seen after.'

—*Beware The Cat,* William Baldwin

Reneé Stockdale / Animals Animals

AN EMERGENCY

His visits to Russell Square, and our expeditions to Cobham where he lived, in the pretty cottage beside the Mole, are marked in memory with a very white stone. The only drawback to the Cobham visits were the 'dear, dear boys'! – i.e. the dachshunds, Max and Geist, who, however adorable in themselves, had no taste for visitors and no intention of letting such intruding creatures interfere with their possession of their master. One would go down to Cobham, eager to talk to 'Uncle Matt' about a book or an article – covetous at any rate of *some* talk with him undisturbed. And it would all end in a breathless chase after Max, through field after field where the little wretch was harrying either sheep or cows, with the dear poet, hoarse with shouting, at his heels. The dogs were always *in the party,* talked to, caressed, or scolded exactly like spoilt children; and the cat of the house was almost equally dear. Once, at Harrow, the then ruling cat – a tom – broke his leg, and the house was in lamentation. The vet was called in, and hurt him horribly. Then Uncle Matt ran up to town, met Professor Huxley at the Athenaeum, and anxiously consulted him. 'I'll go down with you,' said Huxley. The two travelled back instanter to Harrow, and while Uncle Matt held the cat, Huxley – who had begun life, let it be remembered, as Surgeon to the *Rattlesnake!* – examined him, the two black heads together. There is a rumour that Charles Kingsley was included in the consultation. Finally the limb was put in splints, and left to nature. All went well.

—*A Writer's Recollections,* Mrs. Humphrey Ward

THOREAU'S WINGED CAT

Once I was surprised to see a cat walking along the stony shore of the pond, for they rarely wander so far from home. The surprise was mutual. Nevertheless the most domestic cat, which has lain on a rug all her days, appears quite at home in the woods, and, by her sly and stealthy behavior, proves herself more native there than the regular inhabitants. Once, when berrying, I met with a cat with young kittens in the woods, quite wild, and they all, like their mother, had their backs up and were fiercely spitting at me. A few years before I lived in the woods there was what was called a 'winged cat' in one of the farm-houses in Lincoln nearest the pond, Mr. Gilian Baker's. When I called to see her in June, 1842, she was gone a-hunting in the woods, as was her wont, (I am not sure whether it was a male or female, and so use the more common pronoun,) but her mistress told me that she came into the neighborhood a little more than a year before, in April, and was finally taken into their house; that she was of a dark brownish-gray color, with a white spot on her throat, and white feet, and had a large bushy tail like a fox; that in the winter the fur grew thick and flatted out along her sides, forming strips ten or twelve inches long by two and a half wide, and under her chin like a muff, the upper side loose, the under matted like felt, and in the spring these appendages dropped off. They gave me a pair of her 'wings,' which I keep still. There is no appearance of a membrane about them. Some thought it was part flying-squirrel or some other wild animal, which is not impossible, for, according to naturalists, prolific hybrids have been produced by the union of the marten and domestic cat. This would have been the right kind of cat for me to keep, if I had kept any; for why should not a poet's cat be winged as well as his horse?

—*Walden, or, Life in the Woods,* Henry David Thoreau

'THE CAT'

Dear creature by the fire a-purr,
  Strange idol eminently bland,
Miraculous puss! As o'er your fur
  I trail a negligible hand,

And gaze into your gazing eyes,
  And wonder in a demi-dream
What mystery it is that lies
  Behind those slits that glare and gleam,

An exquisite enchantment falls
  About the portals of my sense;
Meandering through enormous halls
  I breathe luxurious frankincense.

An ampler air, a warmer June
  Enfold me, and my wondering eye

Salutes a more imperial moon
  Throned in a more resplendent sky

Than ever knew this northern shore.
  O, strange! For you are with me too,
And I who am a cat once more
  Follow the woman that was you.

With tail erect and pompous march,
  the proudest puss that ever trod,
Through many a grove, 'neath many an arch,
  Impenetrable as a god,

Down many an alabaster flight
  Of broad and cedar-shaded stairs,
While over us the elaborate night
  Mysteriously gleams and glares!

—Lytton Strachey

THE CAT AND THE FOX

The cat and fox, when saints were all the rage,
    Together went on pilgrimage.
Arch hypocrites and swindlers, they,
    By sleight of face and sleight of paw,
    Regardless both of right and law,
Contrived expenses to repay,
By eating many a fowl and cheese,
And other tricks as bad as these.
Disputing served them to beguile
Their road of many a weary mile.
Disputing! but for this resort,
The world would go to sleep, in short.
Our pilgrims, as a thing of course,
Disputed till their throats were hoarse.
    Then, dropping to a lower tone,
They talked of this, and talked of that,
Till Renard whispered to the cat,
    You think yourself a knowing one:
How many cunning tricks have you?
For I've a hundred, old and new,
All ready in my haversack.
The cat replied, I do not lack,
    Though with but one provided
And, truth to honor, for that matter,
I hold it than a thousand better,

In fresh dispute they sided;
And loudly were they at it, when
Approached a mob of dogs and men.
Now, said the cat, your tricks ransack,
And put your cunning brains to rack,
One life to save; I'll show you mine —
A trick, you see, for saving nine.
With that, she climbed a lofty pine.
The fox his hundred ruses tried,
    And yet no safety found.
A hundred times he falsified
    The nose of every hound —
Was here, and there, and every where,
    Above, and under ground;
But yet to stop he did not dare.
Pent in a hole, it was no joke
To meet the terriers or the smoke.
So, leaping into upper air,
He met two dogs, that choked him there.

    Expedients may be too many,
Consuming time to choose and try.
    On one, but that as good as any,
'Tis best in danger to rely.

           —LaFontaine

Reneé Stockdale / Animals Animals

UNCOMMONLY TENDER

Soon after she came back to Haworth [in January 1844], in a letter to one of the household in which she had been staying, there occurs this passage: – 'Our poor little cat has been ill two days, and is just dead. It is piteous to see even an animal lying lifeless. Emily is sorry.' These few words relate to points in the characters of the two sisters, which I must dwell upon a little. Charlotte was more than commonly tender in her treatment of all dumb creatures, and they, with that fine instinct so often noticed, were invariably attracted towards her. The deep and exaggerated consciousness of her personal defects – the constitutional absence of hope, which made her slow to trust in human affection,. and consequently slow to respond to any manifestation of it – made her manner shy and constrained to men and women, and even to children. We have seen something of this trembling distrust of her own capability of inspiring affection, in the grateful surprise she expresses at the regret felt by her Belgian pupils at her departure. But not merely were her actions kind, her words and tones were ever gentle and caressing, towards animals; and she quickly noticed the least want of care or tenderness on the part of others towards any poor brute creature.

—*The Life of Charlotte Brontë,* Mrs. Gaskell

TIBERIUS

Poor Matthias! Woulst thou have
More than pity? claim'st a stave ?
—Friends more near us than a bird
We dismiss'd without a word.
Rover, with the good brown head,
Great Atossa, they are dead;
Dead, and neither prose nor rhyme
Tells the praises of their prime.
Thou didst know them old and grey,
Know them in their sad decay.
Thou hast seen Atossa sage
Sit for hours beside thy cage;
Thou wouldst chirp, thou foolish bird,
Flutter, chirp—she never stirr'd!
What were now these toys to her ?
Down she sank amid her fur;
Eyed thee with a soul resign'd—
And thou deemedst cats were kind!
—Cruel, but composed and bland,
Dumb, inscrutable and grand,
So Tiberius might have sat,
Had Tiberius been a cat.
          —*Poor Matthias,* Matthew Arnold

HODGE

I never shall forget the indulgence with which Dr. Johnson treated Hodge, his cat; for whom he himself used to go out and buy oysters lest the servants, having that trouble, should take a dislike to the poor creature. I am unluckily one of those who have an antipathy to a cat, so that I am uneasy when in the room with one, and I own I frequently suffered a good deal from the presence of the same Hodge.

I recollect him one day scrambling up Dr. Johnson's breast apparently with much satisfaction while my friend smiling and half-whistling, rubbed down his back and pulled him by the tail and when I observed he was a fine cat, saying, "Why yes, sir, but I have had cats that I liked better than this," and then, as if perceiving Hodge to be out of countenance, adding, "but he is a very fine cat, a very fine cat indeed".

This reminds me of the ludicrous account which he gave to Mr. Langton, of the despicable state of a young gentleman of good family. "Sir, when I heard of him last, he was running about town shooting cats". And then in a sort of kindly reverie, he bethought himself of his own favourite cat and said, "But Hodge shan't be shot: no, no, Hodge shall not be shot".

—*Life of Dr. Johnson,* James Boswell

THE INVISIBLE CAT

'**M**y first experiment was with a bit of white wool fabric. It was the strangest thing in the world to see it soft and white in the flicker of the flashes, and then to watch it fade like a wreath of smoke and vanish.

'I could scarcely believe I had done it. I put my hand into the emptiness and there was the thing as solid as ever. I felt it awkwardly, and threw it on the floor. I had a little trouble finding it again.

'And then came a curious experience. I heard a miaow behind me, and turning, saw a lean white cat, very dirty, on the cistern cover outside the window. A thought came into my head. "Everything ready for you," I said, and went to the window, opened it, and called softly. She came in, purring — the poor beast was starving — and I gave her some milk. All my food was in a cupboard in the corner of the room. After that she went smelling round the room, evidently with the idea of making herself at home. The invisible rag upset her a bit; you should have seen her spit at it! But I made her comfortable on the pillow of my truckle-bed, and I gave her butter to get her to wash.'

'And you processed her?'

'I processed her. But giving drugs to a cat is no joke, Kemp! And the process failed.'

'Failed?'

'In two particulars. These were the claws and the pigment stuff — what is it? At the back of the eye in a cat. You know?'

'*Tapetum.*'

'Yes, the *tapetum.* It didn't go. After I'd given the stuff to bleach the blood and done certain other things to her, I gave the beast opium, and put her and the pillow she was sleeping on, on the apparatus. And after all the rest had faded and vanished, there remained the two little ghosts of her eyes.'

'Odd.'

'I can't explain it. She was bandaged and clamped of course — so I had her safe, but she awoke while she was still misty, and miawled dismally, and someone came knocking. It was an old woman from downstairs, who suspected me of vivisecting — a drink-sodden old creature, with only a cat to care for in all the world. I whipped out some chloroform, applied it, and answered the door. "Did I hear a cat?" she asked. "My cat?" "Not here," said I, very politely. She was a little doubtful, and tried to peer past me into the room — strange enough to her, no doubt, bare walls, uncurtained windows, truckle-bed, with the gas-engine vibrating, and the seethe of the radiant points, and the faint stinging of chloroform in the air. She had to be satisfied at last, and went away again.'

'How long did it take?' asked Kemp.

'Three or four hours — the cat. The bones and sinews and the fat were the last to go, and the tips of the coloured hairs. And, as I say, the back part of the eye, tough, iridescent stuff it is, wouldn't go at all.'

—H.G. Wells

Nicholas Devore III / Photographers Aspen

CAT OVERBOARD

The 18. day we abode still at anker, looking for a gale to returne backe, but it was contrary: and the 19. we set saile, but the currant having more force then the winde, we were driven backe, insomuch, that the ship being under saile, we cast the sounding lead, and (notwithstanding the wind) it remained before the shippe, there we hadde muddie ground at fifteen fadome. The same day about 4. of the clocke, wee set saile againe, and sayled West alongst the coast with a fresh side-winde. It chanced by fortune, that the shippes Cat lept into the Sea, which being downe, kept her selfe very valuantly above water, notwithstanding the great waves, still swimming, but which the master knowing, he caused the Skiffe with half a dosen men to goe towards her and fetch her againe, when she was almost halfe a mile from the shippe, and all this while the shippe lay on staies. I hardly believe they would have made such haste and meanes if one of the company had bene in the like perill. They made the more haste because it was the patrons cat. This I have written onely to note the estimation that cats are in, among the Italiana, for generally they esteem their cattes, as in England we esteeme a good Spaniell. The same night about tenne of the clocke the winde calmed, and because none of the shippe knewe where we were, we let fall an anker about 6 mile from the place we were at before, and there wee had muddie ground at twelve fadome.

—*From The Principal Navigations, Voyages, Traffiques and Discoveries of the English Nation,* Richard Hakluyt

DOWN AT HEEL

As the dogs of shy neighbourhoods usually betray a slinking consciousness of being in poor circumstances — for the most part manifested in an aspect of anxiety, an awkwardness in their play, and a misgiving that somebody is going to harness them to something, to pick up a living — so the cats of shy neighbourhoods exhibit a strong tendency to relapse into barbarism. Not only are they made selfishly ferocious by ruminating on the surplus population around them, and on the densely crowded state of all the avenues to cat's meat; not only is there a moral and politico-economical haggardness in them, traceable to these reflections; but they evince a physical deterioration. Their linen is not clean, and is wretchedly got up; their black turns rusty, like old mourning; they wear very indifferent fur; and take to the shabbiest cotton velvet, instead of silk velvet. I am on terms of recognition with several small streets of cats, about the Obelisk in Saint George's Fields, and also in the vicinity of Clerkenwell-green, and also in the back settlements of Drury-lane. In appearance, they are very like the women among whom they live. They seem to turn out of their unwholesome beds into the street, without any preparation. They leave their young families to stagger about the gutters, unassisted, while they frouzily quarrel and swear and scratch and spit, at street corners. In particular, I remark that when they are about to increase their families (an event of frequent recurrence) the resemblance is strongly expressed in a certain dusty dowdiness, down-at-heel self-neglect, and general giving up of things. I cannot honestly report that I have ever seen a feline matron of this class washing her face when in an interesting condition.

—*The Uncommercial Traveller,* Charles Dickens

T. T. T.

It's cooler in there,
The cat is discovering.
Nothing in nature had prepared him for this:
A room dark at midday,
Freezing in summer.

He sniffs the draft
And finds the coldest spot.
Like a building collapsing from the cellar up
He falls floorward in pieces,
And cools like caramel.

—Kid Twist

Nicholas Devore III / Photographers Aspen

SUTTEE OF THE CATS

On every occasion of a fire in Egypt the strangest prodigy occurs with the cats. The inhabitants allow the fire to rage as it pleases, while they stand about at intervals and watch these animals which, slipping by the men or else leaping over them, rush headlong into the flames. When this happens, the Egyptians are in deep affliction. If a cat dies in a private house by a natural death, all the inmates of the house shave their eyebrows. . . . The cats on their decease are taken to the city of Bubastis, where they are embalmed, after which they are buried in certain sacred repositories.

—Herodotus

Sydney Thomson / Animals Animals

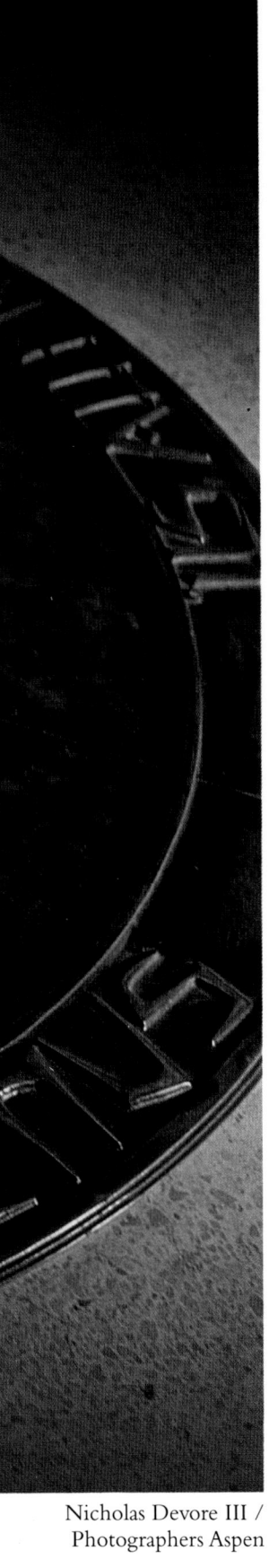

Nicholas Devore III /
Photographers Aspen

CAT AND LADY

They were at play, she and her cat,
And it was marvellous to mark
The white paw and the white hand pat
Each other in the deepening dark.

The stealthy little lady hid
Under her mittens' silken sheath
Her deadly agate nails that thrid
The silk-like dagger points of death.

The cat purred primly and drew in
Her claws that were of steel filed thin:
The devil was in it all the same.

And in the boudoir, while a shout
Of laughter in the air rang out,
Four sparks of phosphor shone like flame.

—Paul Verlaine

Reneé Stockdale / Animals Animals

THE OWL AND THE PUSSY-CAT

The Owl and the Pussy-Cat went to sea
In a beautiful pea-green boat,
They took some honey, and plenty of money,
Wrapped up in a five-pound note.
The Owl looked up to the stars above,
And sang to a small guitar,
"O lovely Pussy! O Pussy, my love,
What a beautiful Pussy you are,
You are,
You are!
What a beautiful Pussy you are!"

Pussy said to the Owl, "You elegant fowl!
How charmingly sweet you sing!
O let us be married! too long we have tarried:
But what shall we do for a ring?"
They sailed away for a year and a day,
To the land where the Bong-tree grows,

And there in a wood a Piggy-wig stood,
With a ring at the end of his nose,
His nose,
His nose,
With a ring at the end of his nose.

"Dear Pig, are you willing to sell for one shilling
Your ring?" Said the Piggy, "I will,"
So they took it away, and were married next day
By the Turkey who lives on the hill.
They dined on mince, and slices of quince,
Which they ate with a runcible spoon;
And hand-in-hand, on the edge of the sand,
They danced by the light of the moon,
The moon,
The moon,
They danced by the light of the moon.

—Edward Lear

THE OLD CAT AND THE YOUNG MOUSE

A young and inexperienced mouse
  Had faith to try a veteran cat, —
  Raminagrobis, death to rat,
And scourge of vermin through the house, —
Appealing to his clemency
  With reasons sound and fair.
Pray let me live; a mouse like me
  It were not much to spare.
Am I, in such a family,
A burden? Would my largest wish
Our wealthy host impoverish?
A grain of wheat will make my meal;
A nut will fat me like a seal.
I'm lean at present: please to wait,
And for your heirs reserve my fate.
  The captive mouse thus spake.
Replied the captor, You mistake;

To me shall such a thing be said?
Address the deaf! address the dead!
A cat to pardon! — old one, too!
Why such a thing I never knew.
  Thou victim of my paw,
  By well-established law,
  Die, as a mousling should,
  And beg the sisterhood,
  Who ply the thread and shears,
  To lend thy speech their ears.
  Some other like repast
  My heirs may find, or fast.
He ceased. The moral's plain.
Youth always hopes its ends to gain,
Believes all spirits like its own:
Old age is not to mercy prone.
          —LaFontaine

Robert Pearcy / Animals Animals

WHICH DREAMED IT?

'Your Red Majesty shouldn't purr so loud,' Alice said, rubbing her eyes, and addressing the kitten, respectfully, yet with some severity. 'You woke me out of oh! such a nice dream; and you've been along with me, Kitty — all through the Looking-Glass world. Did you know it, dear?'

It is a very inconvenient habit of kittens (Alice had once made the remark) that, whatever you say to them, they always purr. 'If they would only purr for "yes," and mew for "no," or any rule of that sort,' she had said, 'so that one could keep up a conversation! But how can you talk with a person if they always say the same thing?'

On this occasion the kitten only purred: and it was impossible to guess whether it meant 'yes' or 'no.'

So Alice hunted among the chessmen on the table till she had found the Red Queen: then she went down on her knees on the hearth-rug, and put the kitten and the Queen to look at each other. 'Now, Kitty!' she cried, clapping her hands triumphantly. 'Confess that was what you turned into!'

('But it wouldn't look at it,' she said, when she was explaining the thing afterwards to her sister: 'it turned away its head, and pretended not to see it: but it looked a little ashamed of itself, so I think it must have been the Red Queen.')

'Sit up a little more stiffly, dear!' Alice cried with a merry laugh. 'And curtsey while you're thinking what to — what to purr. It saves time, remember!' And she caught it up and gave it one little kiss, 'just in honour of its having been a Red Queen.'

'Snowdrop, my pet!' she went on, looking over her shoulder at the White Kitten, which was still patiently undergoing its toilet, 'when will Dinah have finished with your White Majesty, I wonder? That must be the reason you were so untidy in my dream. — Dinah! Do you know that you're scrubbing a White Queen? Really, it's most disrespect-ful of you!

'And what did Dinah turn to, I wonder?' she prattled on, as she settled comfortably down, with one elbow on the rug, and her chin in her hand, to watch the kittens. 'Tell me, Dinah, did you turn to Humpty Dumpty? I think you did — however, you'd better not mention it to your friends just yet, for I'm not sure.

'By the way, Kitty, if only you'd been really with me in my dream, there was one thing you would have enjoyed — I had such a quantity of poetry said to me, all about fishes! To-morrow morning you shall have a real treat. All the time you're eating your breakfast, I'll repeat "The Walrus and the Carpenter" to you; and then you can make believe it's oysters, dear!

'Now, Kitty, let's consider who it was that dreamed it all. This is a serious question, my dear, and you should not go on licking your paw like that — as if Dinah hadn't washed you this morning! You see, Kitty, it must have been either me or the Red King. He was part of my dream, of course — but then I was part of his dream, too! Was it the red King, Kitty? You were his wife, my dear, so you ought to know — Oh, Kitty, do help to settle it! I'm sure your paw can wait!' But the provok-ing kitten only began on the other paw, and pretended it hadn't heard the question.

—*Through The Looking Glass,* Lewis Carroll

THE CAT'S DUTY

The animals, by want oppressed,
To man their services addressed:
While each pursued their selfish good,
They hungered for precarious food:
Their hours with anxious cares were vexed;
One day they fed, and starved the next:
They saw that plenty, sure and rife,
Was found alone in social life;
That mutual industry professed,
The various wants of man redressed.
The cat, half-famished, lean and weak,
Demands the privilege to speak.
'Well, Puss,' says Man, 'and what can you

To benefit the public do?'
The cat replies, 'These teeth, these claws,
With vigilance shall serve the cause,
The mouse destroyed by my pursuit,
No longer shall my feasts pollute;
Nor rats, from mightly ambuscade,
With wasteful teeth your stores invade.'
'I grant,' says man, 'to general use
Your aprts and talents may conduce;
For rats and mice purloin our grain,
And threshers whirl the flail in vain:
Thus shall the cat, a foe to spoil,
Protect the farmer's honest toil.'

—John Gay

Gerard Lacz / Animals Animals

WALTZING CHATTIE

Chattie jumped up on the window-sill, with her usual stealthy *aplomb*, and rubbed herself against the girl's face.

'Oh, Chattie!' cried Rose, throwing her arms around the cat, 'if Catherine'll *only* marry Mr Elsmere, my dear, and be happy ever afterwards, and set me free to live my own life a bit, I'll be *so* good, you won't know me, Chattie. And you shall have a new collar, my beauty, and cream till you die of it!'

And springing up she dragged in the cat, and snatching a scarlet anemone from a bunch on the table, stood opposite Chattie, who stood slowly waving her magnificent tail from side to side, and glaring as though it were not at all to her taste to be hustled and bustled in this way.

'Now, Chattie, listen! Will she?'

A leaf of the flower dropped on Chattie's nose.

'Won't she? Will she? Won't she? Will — Tiresome flower, why did Nature give it such a beggarly few petals? If I'd had a daisy it would have all come right. Come, Chattie, waltz; and let's forget this wicked world!'

And, snatching up her violin, the girl broke into a Strauss waltz, dancing to it the while, her cotton skirts flying, her pretty feet twinkling, till her eyes glowed, and her cheeks blazed with a double intoxication — the intoxication of movement, and the intoxication of sound — the cat meanwhile following her with little mincing perplexed steps as though not knowing what to make of her.

'Rose, you madcap!' cried Agnes, opening the door.

'Not at all, my dear,' said Rose calmly, stopping to take breath. 'Excellent practice and uncommonly difficult. Try if you can do it, and see!'

—*Robert Elsmere*, Mrs. Humphry Ward

DISCORDANT AND HORRID

At the Baron's fee was lying
Gracefully the worthy tom-cat,
Hiddigeigei, with the coal-black
Velvet fur and mighty tail.
'Twas an heirloom from his long-lost,
Much-beloved, and stately consort,
Leonore Monfort de Plessys.
Hiddigeigei's native country
Was Hungaria, and his mother,
Who was of the race Angora
Bore him to a Puszta tom-cat.
In his early youth to Paris
He was sent as a fond token
Of the love of an Hungarian,
Who, though far in Debreczin, still
With due reverence had remembered
The blue eyes of Leonora,
And the rats in her old palace.
With the stately Leonora
To the Rhine came Hiddigeigei.
A true house-pet, somewhat lonesome
Did he while away his life there;
For, he hated to consort with
Any of the German cat-tribe.
'They may have,' thus he was thinking
In his consequential cat-pride,
'Right good hearts, and may possess too
At the bottom some good feeling,

But 'tis polish that is wanting;
A fine culture and high breeding,
I miss sorely in these vulgar
Natives of this forest-city.
And a cat who won his knight spurs
In fair Paris, and who often
In the quarter of Montfaucon
Has enjoyed a racy rat-hunt,
Misses in this little town here
All that is to him congenial,
Any intercourse with equals.'
Isolated, therefore, but still
Ever dignified and solemn
Lived he in this lonely castle.
Graceful through the halls he glided,
Most melodious was his purring;
And in fits of passion even,
When he curved his back in anger,
And his hair stood bristling backward,
Never did he fail to mingle
Dignity with graceful bearing.
But when over roof and gable
Up he softly clambered, starting
On a hunting expedition,
Then mysteriously by moonlight
His green eyes like emeralds glistened;
Then, indeed, he looked imposing
This majestic Hiddigeigei...

So the maiden shyly entered,
Shyly she took up the trumpet,
To her rosy lips she pressed it;
But with fright she well-nigh trembled
At her breath to sound transforming
In the trumpet's golden calyx,
Which the air was bearing farther,
Farther — ah, who knoweth where?
But she cannot stop the fun now,
And with sounds discordant, horrid,
Fit to rend the ears to pieces
So disturbed the morning stillness,
That the poor cat Hiddigeigei's
Long black hair stood up like bristles,
Like the sharp quills of a hedgehog.
Raising then his paw to cover
His offended ear, he spoke thus:
'Suffer on, my valiant cat-heart,
Which so much has borne already,
Also bear this maiden's music!
We, we understand the laws well,
Which do regulate and govern
Sound, enigma of creation.
And we know the charm mysterious
Which invisibly through space floats,
And, intangible a phantom,
Penetrates our hearing organs,
And in beasts' as well as men's hearts
Wakes up love, delight and longing,
Raving madness and wild frenzy.
And yet, we must bear this insult,
That when nightly in sweet mewing
We our love-pangs are outpouring,
Men will only laugh and mock us,
And our finest compositions
Rudely brand as caterwauling.
And in spite of this we witness
That these same fault-finding beings
Can produce such horrid sounds as
Those which I have just now heard.
Are such tones not like a nosegay
Made of straw, and thorns, and nettles,
In the midst a prickly thistle?
And in presence of this maiden
Who the trumpet there is blowing,
Can a man then without blushing
E'er sneer at our caterwauling?
But, thou valiant heart, be patient!
Suffer now, the time will yet come
When this self-sufficient monster,
Man, will steal from us the true art
Of expressing all his feelings;
When the whole world in its struggle
For the highest form of culture
Will adopt our style of music.
For in history, there is justice,
She redresses every wrong.'
                    —*The Trumpeter of Säkkingen*,
                    Joseph Victor von Scheffel

CALVIN: A STUDY OF CHARACTER

His origin and ancestry were shrouded in mystery; even his age was a matter of pure conjecture. Although he was of the Maltese race, I have reason to suppose that he was American by birth, as he certainly was in sympathy. Calvin was given to me eight years ago by Mrs. Stowe, but she knew nothing of his age or origin. He walked into her house one day, out of the great unknown, and became at once at home, as if he had been always a friend of the family. He appeared to have artistic and literary tastes, and it was as if he had inquired at the door if that was the residence of the author of *Uncle Tom's Cabin,* and, upon being assured that it was, had decided to dwell there. This is, of course, fanciful, for his antecedents were wholly unknown; but in his time he could hardly have been in any household where he would not have heard *Uncle Tom's Cabin* talked about. When he came to Mrs. Stowe he was as large as he ever was, and apparently as old as he ever became. Yet there was in him no appearance of age; he was in the happy maturity of all his powers, and you would rather have said in that maturity he had found the secret of perpetual youth. And it was as difficult to believe that he would ever be aged as it was to imagine that he had ever been in immature youth. There was in him a mysterious perpetuity.

The intelligence of Calvin was something phenomenal, in his rank of life. He established a method of communicating his wants and even some of his sentiments; and he could help himself in many things. There was a furnace register in a retired room, where he used to go when he wished to be alone, that he always opened when he desired more heat; but never shut it, any more than he shut the door after himself. He could do almost everything but speak; and you would declare sometimes that you could see a pathetic longing to do that in his intelligent face. I have no desire to overdraw his qualities, but if there was one thing in him more noticeable than another, it was his fondness for nature. He could content himself for hours at a low window, looking into the ravine and at the great trees, noting the smallest stir there; he delighted, above all things, to accompany me walking about the garden, hearing the birds, getting the smell of the fresh earth, and rejoicing in the sunshine. He followed me and gambolled like a dog, rolling over on the turf and exhibiting his delight in a hundred ways. If I worked, he sat and watched me, or looked off over the bank, and kept his ear open to the twitter in the cherry-trees. When it stormed, he was sure to sit at the window, keenly watching the rain or the snow, glancing up and down at its falling; and a winter tempest always delighted him.

—Charles Dudley Warner

MICE BEFORE MILK

Go take a Cat and nourish her with milk
And tender fish, and make her couch of silk,
And let her see a mouse go by the wall,
Anon she waiveth milk and flesh and all
And every dainty which is in the house,
Such appetite hath she to eat the mouse.
Behold the domination here of kind,
Appetite drives discretion from her mind.

— 'The Manciple's Tale,' Geoffrey Chaucer,
transl. William Wordsworth

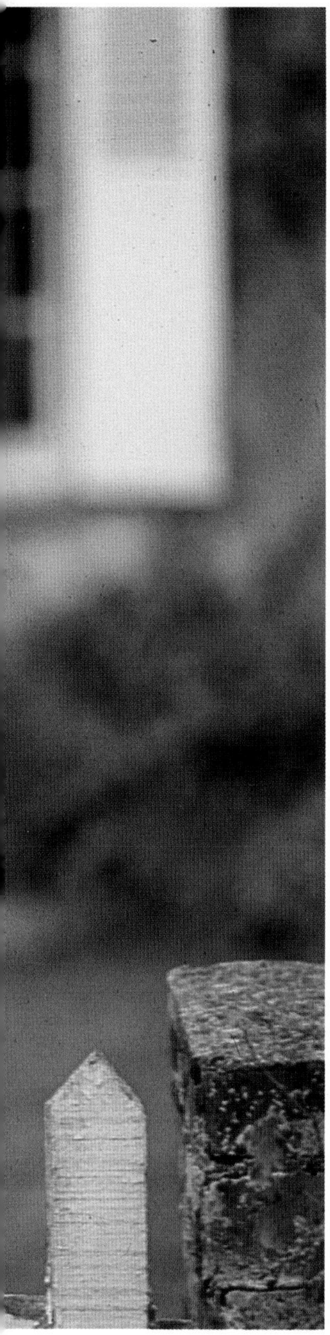

Gerard Lacz /
Animals Animals

Patti Murray / Animals Animals

COLIN CLOUT

Have I not sat with thee full many a night,
When dying embers were our only light,
When every creature did in slumbers lie,
Besides our cat, my Colin Clout, and I?
No troublous thoughts the cat or Colin move,
While I alone am kept awake by love.

—*'The Ditty,'* John Gay

Reneé Stockdale / Animals Animals

THE HIGH BARBAREE

As I was sailing down the coast
   Of High Barbaree,
I chanced to see a Muffin-Bird
   A-sitting in a tree.

Oh, mournfully he sang
   And sorrowful he sat,
Because he was a-frightened of
   The Crum-pet Cat!

The Curmpet Cat is little known;
   He sits him under trees,
And watches for the Muffin Bird
   His palate for to please.

And then he opens wide his mouth
   The cruel Crumpet Cat,
And the Muffin Bird falls into it,
   Just—like—*that!*
                    —Laura E. Richards

THE FOX AND THE CAT

The fox and the cat, as they travell'd one day,
With moral discourses cut shorter the way:
" 'Tis great", says the Fox, "to make justice our guide!"
"How god-like is mercy!" Grimalkin replied.
Whilst thus they proceeded, a wolf from the wood,
Impatient of hunger, and thirsting for blood,
Rush'd forth — as he saw the dull shepherd asleep —
And seiz'd for his supper an innocent sheep.
"In vain, wretched victim, for mercy you bleat,
When mutton's at hand", says the wolf, "I must eat".
Grimalkin's astonish'd — the fox stood aghast,
To see the fell beast at his bloody repast.
"What a wretch", said the cat, " 'tis the vilest of brutes;
Does he feed upon flesh when there's herbage and roots?"

Cries the fox, "While our oaks give us acorns so good'
What a tyrant is this to spill innocent blood!"
Well onward they march'd, and they moraliz'd still,
Till they came where some poultry pick'd chaff by a mill.
Sly Reynard survey'd them with gluttonous eyes,
And made, spite of morals, a pullet his prize.
A mouse, too, that chanced from her covert to stray,
The greedy Grimalkin secured as her prey.
A spider that sat in her web in the wall,
Perceived the poor victims and pitied their fall;
She cried; "Of such murders, how guiltless am I!"
So ran to regale on a new-taken fly.

—J. Cunningham

MY CAT JEOFFRY

For I will consider my Cat Jeoffry.

For he is the servant of the Living God, duly and daily
serving him.

For at the first glance of the glory of God in the East he
worships in his way.

For is this done by wreathing his body seven times round with
elegant quickness.

For then he leaps up to catch the musk, wch is the blessing of
God upon his prayer.

For he rolls upon prank to work it in.

For having done duty and received blessing he begins to consider
himself.

For this he performs in ten degrees.

For first he looks upon his fore-paws to see if they are clean.

For secondly he kicks up behind to clear away there.

For thirdly he works it upon stretch with the forepaws extended.

For fourthly he sharpens his paws by wood.

For fifthly he washes himself.

For sixthly he rolls upon wash.

For seventhly he fleas himself, that he may not be interrupted
upon the beat.

For eighthly he rubs himself against a post.

For ninthly he looks up for his instructions.

For tenthly he goes in quest of food.

For having consider'd God and himself he will consider
his neighbour.

For if he meets another cat he will kiss her in kindness.

For when he takes his prey he plays with it to give it (a) chance.

For one mouse in seven escapes by his dallying.

For when his day's work is done his business more
properly begins.

For keeps the Lord's watch in the night against the adversary.

For he counteracts the powers of darkness by his electrical skin
& glaring eyes.

For he counteracts the Devil, who is death, by brisking about
the life.

For in his morning orisons he loves the sun and the sun
loves him.

For he is of the tribe of Tiger.

For the Cherub Cat is a term of the Angel Tiger.

For he has the subtlety and hissing of a serpent, which in
goodness he suppresses.

For he will not do destruction, if he is well-fed, neither will he
spit without provocation.

For he purrs in thankfulness, when God tells him he's a
good Cat.

For he is an instrument for the children to learn
benevolence upon.

For every house is incompleat without him & a blessing is lacking
in the spirit.

For the Lord commanded Moses concerning the cats at the
departure of the Children of Israel from Egypt.

For every family had one cat at least in the bag.

For the English Cats are the best in Europe.

For he is the cleanest in the use of his forepaws of
any quadrupede.

For the dexterity of his defence is an instance of the love of God
to him exceedingly.

For he is the quickest to his mark of any creature.

For he is tenacious of his point.

For he is a mixture of gravity and waggery.

For he knows that God is his Saviour.

For there is nothing sweeter than his peace when at rest.

For there is nothing brisker than his life when in motion.

For he is of the Lord's poor and so indeed is he called by
benevolence perpetually — Poor Jeoffry! poor Jeoffry!
the rat has bit thy throat.

For I bless the name of the Lord Jesus that Jeoffry is better.

For the divine spirit comes about his body to sustain it in
compleat cat.

For his tongue is exceeding pure so that it has in purity what it
wants in musick.

For he is docile and can learn certain things.

For he can set up with gravity which is patience
upon approbation.

For he can fetch and carry, which is patience in employment.

For he can jump over a stick which is patience upon
proof positive.

For he can spraggle upon waggle at the word of command.

For he can jump from an eminence into his master's bosom.

For he can catch the cork and toss it again.

For he is hated by·the hypocrite and miser.

For the former is affraid of detection.

For the latter refuses the charge.

For he camels his back to bear the first notion of business.

For he is good to think on, if a man would express himself neatly.

For he made a great figure in Egypt for his signal services.

For he killed the Icneumon-rat very pernicious by land.

For his ears are so acute that they sting again.

For from this proceeds the passing quickness of his attention.

For by stroaking of him I have found out electricity.

For I perceived God's light about him both wax and fire.

For the electrical fire is the spiritual substance, which God sends
from heaven to sustain the bodies both of man and beast.

For God has blessed him in the variety of his movements.

For, tho he cannot fly, he is an excellent clamberer.

For his motions upon the face of the earth are more than any
other quadrupede.

For he can tread to all the measures upon the musick.

For he can swim for life.

For he can creep.

—*Rejoice in the Lamb: A Song from Bedlam,*
Christopher Smart

Sydney Thomson / Animals Animals

THE FOSTER-MOTHER

A boy has taken three young squirrels in their nest or drey as it is called in these parts. These small creatures he put under the care of a cat who had lately lost her kittens, and finds that she nurses and suckles them with the same assiduity and affection as if they were her own offspring. This circumstance corroborates my suspicion that the mention of exposed and deserted children being nurtured by female beasts of prey who had lost their young may not be so improbable an incident as many have supposed; and therefore may be a justification of those authors who have gravely mentioned what some have deemed to be a wild and improbable story.

So many people went to see the little squirrels suckled by a cat that the foster-mother became jealous of her charge, and in pain for their safety; and therefore hid them over the ceiling, where one died. This circumstance shows her affection for these fondlings and that she supposes the squirrels to be her own young.

—*Natural History of Selborne,* Gilbert White

THE COMPLEAT ANGLER

Mr. Leonard, a very intelligent friend of mine, saw a cat catch a trout, by darting upon it in a deep clear water, at the mill at Weaford, near Lichfield. The cat belonged to Mr. Stanley, who had often seen her catch fish in the same manner in summer, when the mill-pool was drawn so low that the fish could be seen. I have heard of other cats taking fish in shallow water, as they stood on the bank. This seems to be a natural method of taking their prey, usually lost by domestication, though they all retain a strong relish for fish.

—*The Compleat Angler,* Charles Darwin

Robert Maier / Animals Animals

Sydney Thomson / Animals Animals

THE COLUBRIAD

Close by the threshold of a door nail'd fast,
Three kittens sat; each kitten look'd aghast.
I, passing swift and inattentive by,
At the three kittens cast a careless eye;
Not much concern'd to know what they did there,
Not dreaming kittens worth a poet's ear.
But presently a loud and furious hiss
Caused me to stop, and to exclaim 'What's this?'
When lo! upon the threshold met my view,
With head erect, and eyes of fiery hue,
A viper, long as Count de Grasse's queue.
Forth from his head his forked tongue he throws,
Darting it full against a kitten's nose;
Who never having seen in field or house,
The like, sat still and silent as a mouse:
Only projecting, with attention due,
Her whisker'd face, she asked him, 'Who are you?'
On to the hall went I, with pace not slow,
But swift as light'ning, for a long Dutch hoe:
With which well arm'd I hasten'd to the spot,
To find the viper, but I found him not.

And, turning up the leaves and shrubs around,
Found only, that he was not to be found.
But still the kitten, sitting as before,
Sat watching close the bottom of the door.
'I hope', said I, 'the villain I would kill
Has slipp'd between the door and the door-sill;
And if I make despatch, and follow hard,
No doubt but I shall find him in the yard;
For long ere now it should have been rehearsed
'Twas in the garden that I found him first.
Even there I found him — there the full-grown cat,
His head, with velvet paw, did gently pat;
As curious as the kittens each had been
To learn what this phenomenon might mean.
Fill'd with heroic ardour at the sight,
And fearing every moment he would bite,
And rob our household of our only cat
That was of age to combat with a rat,
With outstretch'd hoe I slew him at the door,
And taught him never to come thither more.'
—William Cowper

THE KITTEN AND THE FALLING LEAVES

That way look, my Infant, lo!
What a pretty baby-show!
See the Kitten on the wall,
Sporting with the leaves that fall,
Withered leaves — one — two — and three —
From the lofty elder-tree!
Through the calm and frosty air
Of this morning bright and fair,
Eddying round and round they sink
Softly, slowly: one might think,
From the motions that are made,
Every little leaf conveyed
Sylph or Faery hither tending, —
To this lower world descending,
Each invisible and mute,
In his wavering parachute.
— But the Kitten, how she starts,
Crouches, stretches, paws, and darts!
First at one, and then its fellow
Just as light and just as yellow;
There are many now — now one —
Now they stop and there are none.
What intenseness of desire
In her upward eye of fire!
With a tiger-leap half-way
Now she meets the coming prey,
Lets it go as fast, and then
Has it in her power again:
Now she works with three or four,
Like an Indian conjurer;
Quick as he in feats of art,
Far beyond in joy of heart.
Were her antics played in the eye
Of a thousand standers-by,
Clapping hands with shout and stare,

What would little Tabby care
For the plaudits of the crowd?
Over happy to be proud,
Over wealthy in the treasure
Of her own exceeding pleasure!
   ★   ★   ★   ★   ★
Such a light of gladness breaks,
Pretty Kitten! from thy freaks, —
Spreads with such a living grace
O'er my little Dora's face;
Yes, the sight so stirs and charms
Thee, Baby, laughing in my arms,
That almost I could repine
That your transports are not mine,
That I do not wholly fare
Even as ye do, thoughtless pair!
And I will have my careless season
Spite of melancholy reason,
Will walk through life in such a way
That, when time brings on decay,
Now and then I may possess
Hours of perfect gladsomeness.
— Pleased by any random toy;
By a kitten's busy joy,
Or an infant's laughing eye
Sharing in the ecstasy;
I would fare like that or this,
Find my wisdom in my bliss;
Keep the sprightly soul awake,
And have faculties to take,
Even from things by sorrow wrought,
Matter for a jocund thought,
Spite of care, and spite of grief,
To gambol with Life's falling Leaf.
—William Wordsworth

THE RAT-CATCHER

The rats by night such mischief did,
Betty was every morning chid:
They undermined whole sides of bacon,
Her cheese was sapped, her tarts were taken;
Her pasties, fenced with thickest paste,
Were all demolished and laid waste:
She cursed the Cat, for want of duty,
Who left her foes a constant booty.
An engineer, of noted skill,
Engaged to stop the growing ill.
From room to room he now surveys
Their haunts, their works, their secret ways;
Finds where they 'scape an ambuscade,
And whence the nightly sally's made.
An envïous Cat from place to place,
Unseen, attends his silent pace:
She saw that, if his trade went on,
The purring race must be undone;
So secretly removes his baits,
And every strategem defeats.
Again he sets the poisoned toils;
And Puss again the labour foils.
"What foe (to frustrate my designs)
My schemes thus nightly countermines?"
Incensed, he cries, "This very hour
The wretch shall bleed beneath my power".
So said, a ponderous trap he brought,
And in the fact poor Puss was caught.
"Smuggler", says he, "thou shalt be made
A victim to our loss of trade".
The captive Cat, with piteous mews,
For pardon, life, and freedom sues.
"A sister of the science spare;
One interest is our common care".
"What insolence!" the man replied;
"Shall cats with us the game divide?
Were all your interloping band
Extinguished, or expelled the land,
We rat-catchers might raise our fees,
Sole guardians of a nation's cheese!"
A Cat, who saw the lifted knife,
Thus spoke, and saved her sister's life.
"In every age and clime we see,
Two of a trade can ne'er agree.
Each hates his neighbour for encroaching:
Squire stigmatizes squire for poaching;
Beauties with beauties are in arms,
And scandal pelts each others' charms;
Kings, too, their neighbour kings dethrone,
In hope to make the world their own;
But let us limit our desires,
Not war like beauties, kings, and squires;
For though we both one prey pursue,
There's game enough for us and you".

—John Gay

WHEN THE CAT IS AWAY, THE MICE MAY PLAY

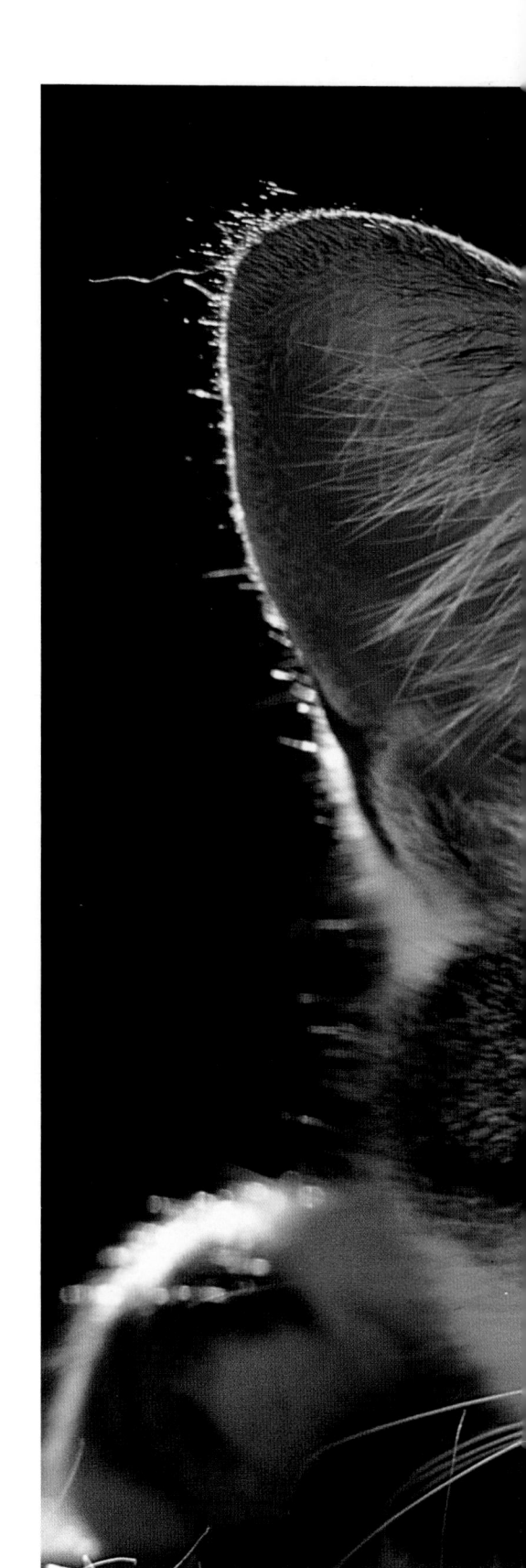

A lady once (so stories say),
By rats and mice infested,
With gins and traps long sought to stay
The thieves; but still they 'scaped away,
And daily her molested.

Great havoc 'mongst her cheese was made,
And much the loss did grieve her:
At length Grimalkin to her aid
She called, (no more of cats afraid),
And begged him to relieve her.

Soon as Grimalkin came in view,
The vermin back retreated;
Grimalkin swift as lightening flew,
Thousands of mice he daily slew,
Thousands of rats defeated.

Ne'er cat before such glory won;
All people did adore him:
Grimalkin far all cats out-shone,
And in his lady's favour none
Was then preferred before him.

Pert Mrs. Abigail alone
Envied Grimalkin's glory:
Her favourite lap-dog now was grown
Neglected; him she did bemoan,
And raved like any Tory.

She cannot bear, she swears she won't,
To see the cat regarded;
But firmly is resolved upon't,
And vows that, whatsoe'er comes on't,
She'll have the cat discarded.

She begs, she storms, she fawns, she frets,
(Her arts are all employed),
And tells her lady in a pet,
Grimalkin cost her more in meat
Than all the rats destroyed.

At length this spiteful waiting-maid
Produced a thing amazing;
The favourite cat's a victim made,
To satisfy this prating jade,
And fairly turned a-grazing.

Now lap-dog is again restored
Into his lady's favour;
Sumptuously kept at bed and board,
And he, (so Nab has given her word),
Shall from all vermin save her.

Nab much exults at this success,
And, overwhelmed with joy,
Her lady fondly does caress,
And tells her, Fubb can do no less
Than all her foes destroy.

But vain such hopes; the mice that fled
Return, now Grim's discarded;
Whilst Fubb till ten, on silken bed,
Securely lolls his drowsy head,
And leaves cheese unregarded.

Nor rats nor mice the lap-dog fear,
Now uncontrolled their theft is:
And whatsoe'er the vermin spare,
Nab and her dog betwixt them share,
Nor pie nor pippin left is.

Meanwhile, to cover their deceit
At once, and slander Grim;
Nab says, the cat comes out of spite,
To rob her lady every night,
So lays it all on him.

Nor corn secure in garret high,
Nor cheese-cake safe in closet;
The cellars now unguarded lie,
On every shelf the vermin prey;
And still Grimalkin does it.

The gains from corn apace decayed,
No bags to market go:
Complaints came from the dairy-maid,
The mice had spoiled her butter trade,
And eke her cheese also.

With this same lady once there lived
A trusty servant-maid,
Who, hearing this, full much was grieved,
Fearing her lady was deceived,
And hastened to her aid.

Much art she used for to disclose
And find out the deceit;
At length she to the lady goes,
Discovers her domestic foes,
And opens all the cheat.

Struck with the sense of her mistake,
The lady, discontented,
Resolves again her cat to take,
And ne'er again her cat forsake,
Lest she again repent it.

—(Ascribed to) Matthew Prior

Joe McDonald / Animals Animals